THE MISSION AND ACHIEVEM

STUDIES IN BIBLICAL THEOLOGY

THE MISSION AND ACHIEVEMENT OF JESUS

*An Examination of the Presuppositions of
New Testament Theology*

REGINALD H. FULLER

*Baldwin Professor of Sacred Literature
Union Theological Seminary
New York*

SCM PRESS LTD
BLOOMSBURY STREET LONDON

TO THE REVERED MEMORY OF MY TEACHERS
EDWYN CLEMENT HOSKYNS
AND
JOHN MARTIN CREED

334 01020 9
First published 1954
by SCM Press Ltd
56 Bloomsbury Street London WC1
Second impression 1956
Third impression 1960
Fourth impression 1963
Fifth impression 1967
Sixth impression 1970

Printed in Great Britain by
Lewis Reprints Limited, Port Talbot, Glamorgan

CONTENTS

PREFACE

THE sub-title of this little book was suggested by the opening sentence of Dr. Rudolf Bultmann's *Theology of the New Testament* (1952): 'The message of Jesus is a presupposition for the theology of the New Testament rather than a part of that theology itself.' If the foundation of New Testament theology is the *kerygma* of the Church, that statement may be allowed to stand. For the message of Jesus, and indeed his whole life's mission, form the basis from which the *kerygma* sprang. The thesis of this book however is that the presuppositions, as outlined by Dr. Bultmann, are inadequate to account for the *kerygma*, and its purpose is to propose a more adequate interpretation of the history of Jesus to put in its place.

This critique of the opening chapter of Dr. Bultmann's work has grown out of the first of three lectures delivered to the School for Junior Clergy of the Church in Wales at St. David's College, Lampeter in September 1951. These lectures were a preview of Dr. Bultmann's work prior to its publication in English. Since then the work has been published, and the issues here raised are even more relevant than they were at the time when the lectures were first delivered.

I am indebted to the Reverend Canon H. K. Archdall, at that time Principal of St. David's College, for encouraging me to work up my material into publishable form, as well as to the Venerable J. O. Cobham, lately Principal of the Queen's College at Birmingham, and to Dr. Floyd V. Filson and readers of the S.C.M. Press for reading the typescript and suggesting a number of amendments. My indebtedness to the Reverend Professor H. F. D. Sparks of Oxford University is also acknowledged at one point in the text.

REGINALD H. FULLER

St. David's College
Lampeter
September 1953

PREFACE TO THE SECOND EDITION

A FEW minor misprints have been corrected and a few extra references to other literature have been added. I am indebted to the Reverend Doctors R. P. C. Hanson and John A. T. Robinson for calling my attention to some of these misprints.

A suggestion from Professor Joachim Jeremias of Göttingen has enabled me to strengthen the argument on p. 81, footnote 2. Professor Jeremias has further assured me that he concurs with my view that St. Paul "received" the tradition of the Lord's Supper at his conversion, though the version reproduced in 1 Cor. 11. 23-25 represents a later recension. This of course must have been the case if Mark 14. 25-27 is closer to the Aramaic original than the Pauline version.

REGINALD H. FULLER

Seabury-Western Theological Seminary
  Evanston, Illinois
    October 1955

LIST OF ABBREVIATIONS

BARRETT, *Spirit* = *The Holy Spirit and the Gospel Tradition*, by C. K. Barrett, 1947.

BIENECK, *Sohn Gottes* = *Sohn Gottes als Christusbezeichnung der Synoptiker*, by Joachim Bieneck, 1951.

BLUNT, *Mark* = *The Gospel according to St. Mark* (Clarendon Series), by A. W. F. Blunt, 1929.

BULTMANN, *Theology* = *Theology of the New Testament* Vol. I, by Rudolf Bultmann, 1952 (Tr. from German of 1948).

BULTMANN, *Tradition* = *Die Geschichte der synoptischen Tradition*, by Rudolf Bultmann, ^{2}1931.

CREED, *Luke* = *The Gospel according to St. Luke*, by John Martin Creed, 1930.

CULLMANN, *Baptism* = *Baptism in the New Testament*, by Oscar Cullmann, 1950 (Tr. from German of 1948).

DALMAN, *Jesus-Jeshuah* = *Jesus-Jeshuah*, by Gustaf Dalman, 1929 (Tr. from German of 1921).

DIBELIUS, *Tradition* = *From Tradition to Gospel*, by Martin Dibelius, 1934 (Tr. from German of 1933).

DODD, *Apostolic Preaching* = *The Apostolic Preaching and Its Developments*, by C. H. Dodd, 1936.

DODD, *Parables* = *The Parables of the Kingdom*, by C. H. Dodd, 1935.

DODD, *Scriptures* = *According to the Scriptures*, by C. H. Dodd, 1952.

E.T. = *Expository Times*.

LEMINGTON, *Baptism* = *The New Testament Doctrine of Baptism*, by W. F. Flemington, 1948.

FLEW, *Church* = *Jesus and His Church*, by R. Newton Flew, 1938.

HARNACK, *Sayings* = *The Sayings of Jesus*, by Adolf Harnack, 1908 (Tr. from German of 1907).

HIGGINS, *Lord's Supper* = *The Lord's Supper in the New Testament*, by A. J. B. Higgins, 1951.

HOSKYNS and DAVEY, *Riddle* = *The Riddle of the New Testament*, by Sir Edwyn Hoskyns and Noel Davey, 1931.

JACKSON and LAKE, *Beginnings* = *The Beginnings of Christianity*, edited by F. L. Foakes Jackson and Kirsopp Lake. Part I, Vols. I-V, 1920-1933.

JEREMIAS, *Abendmahlsworte* = *Die Abendmahlsworte Jesu*, by Joachim Jeremias, ²1949.

JEREMIAS, *Jesusworte* = *Unbekannte Jesusworte*, by Joachim Jeremias, 1951.

JEREMIAS, *Kindertaufe* = *Hat die Urkirche die Kindertaufe geübt?*, by Joachim Jeremias, ²1949.

J.T.S. = *Journal of Theological Studies*.

Kerygma and Myth = *Kerygma and Myth*. Edited by H. W. Bartsch, 1953 (Tr. from German of 1948).

KLOSTERMANN, *Mark* = *Das Markusevangelium*, by Ernst Klostermann, ²1926.

KLOSTERMANN, *Matthew* = *Das Matthäusevangelium*, by Ernst Klostermann, ²1927.

KÜMMEL, *Verheissung* = *Verheissung und Erfüllung*, by W. G. Kümmel, ²1953.

LAMPE, *Seal* = *The Seal of the Spirit*, by G. W. H. Lampe, 1950.

MANSON, *Teaching* = *The Teaching of Jesus*, by T. W. Manson, 1931.

MANSON, *Messiah* = *Jesus the Messiah*, by W. Manson, 1943.

Mysterium Christi = *Mysterium Christi*. Edited by G. K. A. Bell and Adolf Deissmann, 1938 (Tr. from German of 1934).

OTTO, *Kingdom* = *The Kingdom of God and the Son of Man*, by Rudolf Otto, 1938 (Tr. from German of 1934).

RAWLINSON, *Mark* = *St. Mark*, by A. E. J. Rawlinson (Westminster Commentary), 1925.

RAWLINSON, *Christ* = *The New Testament Doctrine of the Christ*, by A. E. J. Rawlinson, 1926.

RENGSTORF, *Luke* = *Das Evangelium nach Lukas* (N. T. Deutsch, Vol. III), by Karl Heinrich Rengstorf, ⁶1952.

RICHARDSON, *Miracles* = *The Miracle Stories of the Gospels*, by Alan Richardson, 1941.

SCHLATTER, *Matthew* = *Der Evangelist Matthäus*, by Adolf Schlatter, ³1948.

List of Abbreviations

SCHNIEWIND, *Mark = Das Evangelium nach Markus* (N. T. Deutsch, Vol. I), by Julius Schniewind, [5]1949.

SCHNIEWIND, *Matthew = Das Evangelium nach Matthäus* (N. T. Deutsch, Vol. II), by Julius Schniewind, [6]1951.

TAYLOR, *Mark = The Gospel according to St. Mark*, by Vincent Taylor, 1952.

TAYLOR, *Sacrifice = Jesus and His Sacrifice*, by Vincent Taylor, 1952.

TAYLOR, *Tradition = Formation of the Gospel Tradition*, by Vincent Taylor, 1935.

T.W.N.T. = *Theologisches Wörterbuch zum Neuen Testament*, Vols. I-IV. Edited by Gerhard Kittel; Vol. V, *Lieferungen* 1-12, edited by Gerhard Friedrich, 1933-1954.

Word Book = A Theological Word Book of the Bible. Edited by Alan Richardson, 1950.

I

INTRODUCTORY

1. THE RIDDLE

IN 1931 Sir Edwyn Hoskyns and the Reverend F. N. Davey opened their *Riddle of the New Testament* with some striking words which have since become almost classic:

> When the Catholic Christian kneels at the words *incarnatus est* or at the words *and was incarnate*, he marks with proper solemnity his recognition that the Christian religion has its origin not in general religious experience, nor in some peculiar esoteric mysticism, nor in a dogma. He declares his faith to rest upon a particular event in history. . . . This is Christian orthodoxy, both Catholic and Protestant. In consequence the Christian religion is not merely open to historical investigation, but demands it, and its piety depends on it. Inadequate or false reconstruction of Jesus of Nazareth cuts at the heart of Christianity.

This—the connexion between the Jesus of History on the one hand, and the proclamation by the early Church of Jesus as the event of redemption on the other hand—was the riddle of the New Testament in 1931, and it is still the riddle of the New Testament twenty years after. The *kerygma* of the primitive Church, which has been recovered for us by New Testament scholars during the last thirty years,[1] presents a particular redemptive interpretation of an historical event or series of events, and the crucial problem is whether this interpretation was arbitrarily imposed upon the events subsequently to their occurrence, or whether the events were such as to demand that interpretation—or, even more precisely, did they bear that interpretation in the mind of the central figure of those events, Jesus of Nazareth himself?

[1] See esp. Dodd, *Apostolic Preaching*.

13

2. BULTMANN'S CHALLENGE

In an essay published in 1941, Dr. Rudolf Bultmann[1] contended among other things that the *kerygma* of the New Testament is an attempt of the early Church to interpret the very earthly history of Jesus of Nazareth as the redemptive event by the use of mythological terminology. Bultmann makes it quite clear that while he himself personally accepts the redemptive significance attached to the event of Jesus, yet the history of Jesus does not itself disclose or demand that significance. In speaking of the Resurrection[2] he says: 'It would be wrong at this point to raise again the problem of how this preaching arose historically. *That would be to tie our faith to the results of historical research.* The word of preaching confronts us as the Word of God. It is not for us to question its credentials. It is we who are questioned, we who are asked whether we will believe the word or reject it' (italics mine). Bultmann has here a twofold concern. One is, that nothing must be done to weaken what he calls the *Nichtausweisbarkeit*, the 'unproveability' of the Christian proclamation. If it could be proved, faith would be deprived of its essential *scandalon*, and robbed of its character as decision. The other concern is that faith must not be delivered over to the vagaries and vicissitudes of historical criticism. Now this twofold concern of Bultmann is certainly a legitimate one. Even if for instance it can be proved that Jesus claimed himself to be the redemptive act of God that cannot prove that he is so. There are limits to what the historian can do, as was recognized by Hoskyns and Davey at the conclusion of their *Riddle*: 'The historian can outline the historical figure of Jesus of Nazareth. . . . Upon the ultimate question of truth and falsehood he is unable, as an historian, to decide. . . . Here, then, the historian is driven to lay down his pen, not because he is defeated; not because his material has proved incapable of historical treatment, but because at this point, he is faced by the problem of theology, just as at this same point the unbeliever is faced by the problem of faith.' Yet Hoskyns was careful to maintain that the

[1] Eng. Trans., 'New Testament and Mythology' in *Kerygma and Myth*.
[2] *Op. cit.*, p. 4.

historian has a legitimate though limited function to perform, albeit of a preliminary and preparatory character, in relation to the decision of faith. Bultmann's kind of *entweder oder* may appeal to the Germanic mind, but the practical-minded Englishman in the street, and the scholarly Englishman brought up by his classical training to believe that faith and reason cannot be thus divorced, suspect that there is a catch in it somewhere. To believe that Jesus of Nazareth and his fate are the saving act of God in history involves a particular interpretation of a particular track of history, and it is therefore of primary importance for the decision of faith to know whether that history can bear the weight of that interpretation. Was that interpretation imposed arbitrarily upon those events by the first Christians, or was that history such as to demand that interpretation? More than that, did the chief actor in them give those events a different interpretation from that which the early Church subsequently gave them? If the answer to this last question be in the affirmative, it will follow that the Church knew better than Jesus himself the meaning of what he was doing, and if that be so, there will be no limit to the 'decisions of faith' which it will be entitled to ask from us. What is to prevent the Church from asking us to accept, e.g. the dogma of the Assumption of the Blessed Virgin Mary, or indeed to swallow anything else it may choose to produce from the conjuror's hat? Or again, why should the Church have selected just this particular track of history and have proclaimed it to be the redemptive act of God? Why not—a very pertinent question, in view of the nature of Bultmann's reconstruction of the history of Jesus—the history of John the Baptist, who was also an eschatological prophet and died a martyr's death? Hoskyns was surely right: 'False or inadequate reconstruction of the history of Jesus of Nazareth cuts at the very heart of Christianity.'

3. BULTMANN'S JESUS

Bultmann's reconstruction of the history of Jesus will be found in a conveniently accessible form in Chapter I of his *Theology*. This chapter presents in summary, and in rather dogmatic form, the results of his earlier scientific work, *Die Geschichte der synoptischen Tradition* ([1]1921, [2]1931) and of his more popular *Jesus* (1929, Eng. Trans. *Jesus and the Word*, 1934). Many English scholars have dealt with particular points in Bultmann's reconstruction.[1] But in view of the recent appearance of his *Theology* in English, the time seems ripe for a general consideration of his reconstruction.

Let us briefly summarize the reconstruction Bultmann gives us of the history of Jesus.[2] Jesus appears on the stage of human history as a prophet who announces the impending advent of the Reign of God (p. 4). This Reign, or Kingdom, is interpreted exclusively in terms of the cosmic eschatology of Jewish apocalyptic. It is dawning (*im Anbruch*), but *it is not yet already present*. '*All this does not mean that God's Reign is already here; but it does mean that it is dawning*' (p. 7—italics Bultmann's). The decisive irruption is still in the future: the view 'that Jesus saw the *presence* of God's Reign in his own person and in the followers who gathered about him . . . cannot be substantiated. . . . On the contrary, Jesus clearly *expected the irruption* of God's Reign as a miraculous, world-transforming event' (p. 22—italics mine). Bultmann has chosen his language with extreme care. He distinguishes carefully between what he calls the dawn (*Anbruch*) of God's Reign, and the irruption (*Hereinbrechen*) of it. The first is already taking place when Jesus steps forth into the plane of history, the second he announces and awaits as a cosmic event. He points to the first as a sign of the impending arrival of the second. His ministry takes place as it were in the interval between the first light and the sunrise. The dawn is already taking place in the period of his activity. The irruption however, is, during that activity, a *future* event. In face of this future event Jesus summons men to a radical decision. Bultmann concedes that the person of Jesus is bound up with his proclamation (p. 9), for Jesus is in his own person the sign of the impending event. The fact that he is there is a sign that the Reign of God is dawning and that its irruption is imminent. Thus the decision which Jesus demands is already a decision

[1] e.g. W. Manson, *Messiah*; Rawlinson, *Mark*; Taylor, *Sacrifice* and *Mark*.
[2] The page numbers throughout this paragraph refer to Bultmann's *Theology*.

about his person, though not as the bringer of the Reign of God, but only as the bearer of the word of its imminence. Jesus did not claim to be himself the Messiah, the agent through whom God was actually bringing in, or would in the very near future bring in, his eschatological Reign (pp. 26 ff). He claimed only to be a part of its dawning, a sign of the coming Reign.

It was only after the Resurrection that the Church identified Jesus with the bringer of the eschatological salvation. As a result of the impact of the Resurrection appearances (the historicity of which as subjective experiences of the first disciples Bultmann is prepared to concede)[1] the early Church proceeded to interpret Jesus' claim to be a sign of the coming Reign to mean that he was himself the agent of its inauguration, in fact the Messiah. And therefore in the Synoptic Gospels, and still more radically in the Fourth Gospel, the traditional material about the history of Jesus has been reshaped so as to make Jesus appear already in his lifetime as the Messiah.

The Grounds of Bultmann's Reconstruction

The starting point for this radical reconstruction of the history of Jesus is that the Christian proclamation in its earliest recoverable form dated the inauguration of the Messiahship of Jesus neither from eternity nor from his Birth or Baptism, but from his Resurrection (p. 26). This is clear from certain kerygmatic passages in the Acts and in the Epistles:

Let all the house of Israel therefore know assuredly that God hath made him both Lord and Christ, this Jesus whom ye crucified (Acts 2.36).

. . . who was declared to be the Son of God with power, according to the spirit of holiness by the resurrection of the dead (Rom. 1.4).

Wherefore [i.e. because of and subsequently to his life of humiliation and obedience which culminated in the passion, vv. 7-8] also God highly exalted him, and gave him the name which is above every name [i.e. the name of Messiah, KYRIOS CHRISTOS, v. 11] (Phil. 2.9).

[1] See *Kerygma and Myth*, pp. 38 ff.

This indisputable evidence from the earliest recoverable proclamation is buttressed by certain supposedly assured results
from the form-critical analysis of the gospel tradition. It is,
as is well known, the belief of the form critics that the *pericopae*
or units of material which form the bulk of the Synoptic
Gospels (apart from the generalizing summaries and the Passion
narratives) all existed in the stage of oral transmission in isolated fragments, and that therefore the order in which the
evangelists placed them is due entirely to the evangelists
themselves. Hence it is quite possible (and Bultmann considers it certain, p. 26) that Peter's Confession at Caesarea
Philippi and the Transfiguration are misplaced Resurrection
stories. Consequently Peter's confession 'Thou art the Christ'
referred originally not to the earthly Jesus, but to the glorified
Jesus after the Resurrection. The same applies also to the
Voice from Heaven at the Transfiguration: 'This is my beloved
Son.' Thus, in their original context, these two events bear
witness to a belief, already testified in the earliest *kerygma*, that
the Messiahship of Jesus dated only from the Resurrection.
The narrative of the Baptism of Jesus and the Q version of
the Temptation, both of which assert the divine Sonship of
Jesus in his earthly life, belong to a later stage in the development of the oral tradition than the Petrine Confession and the
Transfiguration, for they represent the theology not of the
earliest (Aramaic) *kerygma*, but that of the Hellenistic churches,
who interpreted Jesus as a 'divine man'. Thus they are not
misplaced Resurrection stories, but 'legends', i.e. stories
which, whatever their original basis in fact, have been shaped
beyond recovery to express the Church's developing faith that
Jesus was Messiah already on earth (26 f).

The only important Christological texts which remain for
Bultmann to dispose of are the Son of Man passages (p. 30).
Apart from those cases where it is simply a mistranslation of
the Aramaic *băr nāshā'* = 'man' or 'I', they fall into two classes:
those which predict the suffering of the Son of Man, and
those which predict a triumphant Son of Man coming from
heaven at the End. Both types are found in Mark, but only the
second type in Q, and Mark never conflates the two types: the

Parousia predictions are quite distinct and independent of the Passion predictions and *vice versa*. An examination of the Passion predictions makes it clear that they are *vaticinia ex eventu*. The Parousia predictions appear both in Mark and in Q, which shows that they belong to an early tradition, and, Bultmann thinks, are probably authentic sayings of Jesus. In these sayings, however, Jesus does not identify himself with this coming Son of Man, but speaks of that figure as one distinct from himself. Indeed, according to Bultmann, it is quite impossible that Jesus should have identified himself with the apocalyptic Son of Man. For Jesus stood among men as a rabbi, prophet and wonder-worker, and there could be no connecting link between him and the figure coming on the clouds of heaven (p. 29). The frequently repeated assertion that his suffering was to supply the link falls to the ground, and the equally common assumption that Jesus by a deliberate and creative reinterpretation of Messianic doctrine conflated the Isaianic suffering servant with the apocalyptic Son of Man also breaks down in the light of hard facts (p. 31). For the Passion predictions have nothing to do with the Parousia predictions: they belong to a later stratum of the tradition, and are in fact the editorial creations of Mark; otherwise there is no trace of any influence of Isa. 53 in the indubitably authentic *logia* of Jesus (p. 31).

Mark's Gospel thus represents the attempt of Hellenistic Christians to impose a Christology on an originally un-Christological history, and Bultmann adopts Wrede's theory of the Messianic secret to account for Mark's handling of his still patently un-Christological material (p. 32). By this device Mark reconciles the earlier post-Resurrection Christology with the later Christological conceptions of Hellenistic Christianity.

II

THE KINGDOM OF GOD
IN THE PROCLAMATION
OF JESUS

1. THE IMMINENCE OF THE KINGDOM

IT must be said at the outset that Bultmann's treatment of the Kingdom of God in the proclamation of Jesus merits more serious consideration than this interpretation often receives in this country. For it is widely held that Jesus proclaimed already in his lifetime a 'realized eschatology'.[1] With the appearance of Jesus, we are to suppose, the eschatological Reign of God had actually entered into history: the Kingdom of God had come. 'The *eschaton* has moved from the future to the present, from the sphere of expectation into that of realized experience.'[2] No doubt the Reign of God awaits consummation somewhere beyond the bounds of history. Dr. Dodd apparently would place this, as far as the individual is concerned, on the other side of his individual death: 'But the spirit of man, though dwelling in history, belongs to the eternal order [a Platonic, rather than biblical idea] and the full meaning of the Day of the Son of Man, or the Kingdom of God, he can experience only in the eternal order.'[3] For the rest, the futurist apocalyptic imagery in the gospels, so far as it is accepted as authentic to Jesus, and not the product of the

---

[1] This term was apparently first used by Dr. C. H. Dodd in *Parables*, p. 51, and the theory which it denotes first popularized by him in Chapter II of that work. Dr. Dodd claims the support of R. Otto's *Reich Gottes und Menschensohn* (1934 Eng. Trans. *The Kingdom of God and the Son of Man*)—see especially *Parables*, p. 49, footnote 1. There is however in Otto's work a strong sense of the future aspect to which Dodd fails to do justice. Cf. especially Otto, *Kingdom*, p. 59: 'Jesus preached: The time is fulfilled. The end is near at hand.... So near that one is tempted to translate: It is present.... *From its futurity it extends its operation into the present*' (italics mine). See also Dodd in E.T. XLVIII, pp. 138 ff. The theory of 'realized eschatology' has been widely adopted despite the searching linguistic criticisms of Professor J. Y. Campbell (*ibid.*, pp. 91 f) and J. M. Creed (*ibid*, pp. 184 f). See e.g. Richardson, *Miracles*, Chapter III; Taylor, *Sacrifice*, p. 11, and, with reservations, *Mark*, pp. 114 ff, pp. 166 f; Flew, *Church*, pp. 31 f, with reservations.
[2] Dodd, *Parables*, p. 50.   [3] *Ibid.*, p. 108.

Church's theology, is dismissed as 'an accommodation of language'.[1]

Four principal texts have been adduced in support of this thesis: (1) Mark 1.15 (cf. Matt. 10.7 = Luke 10.9); (2) Matt. 12.28 = Luke 11.20; (3) Mark 9.1; (4) Luke 17.21. Professor J. Y. Campbell (see p.20, footnote 1) has submitted Dr. Dodd's linguistic arguments to a searching analysis, to which the reader is referred. Here are some further points for consideration.

(1) Mark 1.15 (cf. Matt. 10.7 = Luke 10.9): ἤγγικεν ἡ βασιλεία τοῦ θεοῦ.

Dr. Dodd would translate 'The Kingdom of God has come'.[2] Professor Campbell[3] has shown that in the LXX ἐγγίζω in the majority of cases denotes 'to draw nigh', although on occasion it may be stretched to mean 'reached', as for example in the passage adduced by Dodd,[4] Jonah 3.6 (ἤγγισεν ὁ λόγος πρὸς τὸν βασιλέα), but in each exceptional case the context makes the meaning quite clear. In profane usage the verb is rare in Hellenistic Greek. H. Preisker[5] notes one instance where it bears a transitive sense = to bring nigh, and eight instances where it is intransitive (including three cases from the papyri where it means 'to draw nigh' or 'to approach'). Liddell and Scott (1940) give no case where it means 'to arrive'. In the New Testament the verb ἐγγίζω occurs thirty-five times apart from the cases where ἡ βασιλεία τοῦ θεοῦ (τῶν οὐρανῶν) is the subject. Of these, twenty-four refer to spatial motion, literal or metaphorical, and in each case may be translated 'to draw nigh' or 'to approach'. It is the remaining occurrences referring to time which interest us here.

(i) Matt. 21.34: ὅτε δὲ ἤγγισεν ὁ καιρὸς τῶν καρπῶν
R.V.: 'and when the season of the fruits drew near'

This could be translated 'when the season of fruits had arrived', but the normal profane sense 'drew nigh' makes perfectly good sense—the servants are sent from 'another

---

[1] Dodd, *Parables*, p. 108.   [2] *Ibid.*, pp. 44 f.
[3] See p. 20, footnote 1.   [4] E.T., *loc. cit.*   [5] T.W.N.T., II, p. 329.

country' (verse 33) well in advance, so as to be in time to receive the fruits.[1]

(ii) Matt. 26.45: ἰδοὺ ἤγγικεν ἡ ὥρα
R.V.: 'the hour is at hand'

Since the Markan original had ἦλθεν ἡ ὥρα (Mark 14.41), this may be an instance where the meaning has been stretched, as in Jonah 3.6 (see above). It is more likely, however, that Matthew has deliberately intended to correct Mark. The ὥρα is not the arrest, but the death of Jesus.[2]

(iii) Luke 21.8: ὁ καιρὸς ἤγγικεν
R.V.: 'the time is at hand'

The disciples have asked in verse 7 for the sign that 'these things' (presumably the End) are about to come to pass. Jesus warns them about a false sign—the false prophets who come in his name claiming themselves to be the sign that 'these things' are about to come to pass. The false prophets would therefore claim that the End is near, has drawn nigh, not that it 'has come'—it would be too late then to talk about signs of the approaching End!

(iv) Luke 21.20: ἤγγικεν ἡ ἐρήμωσις αὐτῆς
R.V.: 'her desolation is at hand'

The beleaguering of the city must obviously precede its destruction, and therefore the translation of the R.V. is the only possible one.

(v) Luke 21.28: ἐγγίζει ἡ ἀπολύτρωσις ὑμῶν
R.V.: 'your redemption draweth nigh'

R.V. is obviously correct here, as the first part of the verse shows: 'when these things *begin* to come to pass.'

(vi) Luke 22.1: ἤγγισεν δὲ ἡ ἑορτὴ τῶν ἀζύμων
R.V.: 'now the feast of unleavened bread drew nigh'

The Markan parallel has ἦν δὲ τὸ πάσχα καὶ τὰ ἄζυμα μετὰ δύο

---

[1] Cf. Kümmel, *Verheissung*, pp. 16 ff, to whose examination of ἐγγίζω I am much indebted in this section.   [2] Cf. Kümmel, *Verheissung*, p. 16.

ἡμέρας,[1] and verse 7 shows that Luke clearly does not intend to change the Markan dating ('and the day of unleavened bread came'—ἦλθεν—subsequently to the meeting of the Sanhedrin).

(vii) Acts 7.17.: καθὼς δὲ ἤγγιζεν ὁ χρόνος τῆς ἐπαγγελίας
R.V.: 'but as the time of promise drew nigh'
The 'time of promise' is the Exodus, and the growth of the Hebrew population obviously preceded the Exodus. R.V. is clearly right.

(viii) Rom. 13.12: ἡ δὲ ἡμέρα ἤγγικεν
R.V.: 'the day is at hand'
This follows the clause 'The night is far spent', and is obviously a case of synonymous parallelism. If the night is far spent, the day cannot yet have arrived. R.V. is correct.

(ix) Heb. 10.25: ὅσῳ βλέπετε ἐγγίζουσαν τὴν ἡμέραν
R.V.: 'as ye see the day drawing nigh'
R.V. is clearly right here.

(x) Jas. 5.8: ὅτι ἡ παρουσία τοῦ κυρίου ἤγγικεν
R.V.: 'the coming of the Lord is at hand'
The immediately preceding exhortation 'be patient' makes it perfectly clear that the Parousia is a *future* event for which the faithful must *wait*. R.V. is correct.

(xi) 1 Pet. 4.7: πάντων δὲ τὸ τέλος ἤγγικεν
R.V.: 'the end of all things is at hand'
The *imminence* of the End is made the ground of ethical exhortation. If the End had already come, the time for ethical exhortation would be past! Once more, R.V. is correct.

It is clear from the foregoing analysis that in every other instance (apart from Mark 1.15 and Matt. 10.7 = Luke 10.9 which are under consideration) the verb ἐγγίζω is used of events which have not yet occurred, but which lie in the proximate future. It would therefore be surprising if the word bore a different sense at Mark 1.15 and Matt. 10.7 = Luke 10.9. It might of course still be argued, as Dr. Dodd has argued, that the verb here bore the exceptional sense 'has arrived' as

[1] Mark 14. 1.

at Jonah 3.6. But, as was already noted, the exceptional meaning is determined by the context. And the context does not demand the exceptional meaning here. Had the evangelists required the exceptional meaning, they would doubtless have used a wholly unambiguous verb such as ἦλθεν. Thus we conclude that the phrase ἤγγικεν ἡ βασιλεία τοῦ θεοῦ speaks of an event which, *though near, still lies in the future*.

But this is not the whole story. The background of the synoptic use of ἐγγίζω in relation to the Kingdom of God is derived from the use of that word in Deutero-Isaiah.[1]

Here we find the verb ἐγγίζω used to translate the Heb. *qārābh*:

He is near that justifieth me (Isa. 50.8).

Heb. *qārôbh māçdîqî*.

LXX ἐγγίζει ὁ δικαιώσας με

My righteousness is near (Isa. 51.5).

Heb. *qārôbh çidhqî*.

LXX ἐγγίζει τάχυ ἡ δικαιοσύνη μου

My salvation is near to come (Isa. 56.1).

Heb. (*ki*) *qᵉrôbhā yᵉshûᶜāthî lābhôʾ*.

LXX ἤγγισεν γὰρ τὸ σωτήριόν μου παραγίνεσθαι (AQ. *vl*,
    Bℵ: ἤγγικεν).

It is to be noted that in each case the Hebrew uses a present participle (*qārôbh* = is approaching, incompleted action), while the LXX oscillates between the present and the aorist. Indeed, at Isa. 56.1 there is excellent MSS. support for the perfect ἤγγικεν, exactly as in the gospel passages under consideration, though this isolated instance should not be pressed. This does, however, suggest that we are entitled to give the perfect ἤγγικεν in Mark 1.15, etc., the same dynamic, present meaning which the Hebrew present participle has in the passages cited above. Now the 'righteousness' and 'salvation', whose approach Deutero-Isaiah announces, is the impending act of God in the event of the return from exile. That decisive event has not

[1] Cf. H. Preisker in T.W.N.T., II, p. 330.

yet occurred. But—and this is the important point—that event is already so near that it is operative in advance in the preliminary victories of Cyrus (Isa. 41.25, etc.). These preliminary victories are signs of the coming restoration, but signs organically connected with it. For the signs are produced by the same energy and power which is to produce the decisive event. We must therefore expand the connotation of ἤγγικεν at Mark 1.15, etc. While it still asserts that the decisive event, though impending, still lies in the future, it means more than that. It has the same dynamic force as *qarobh*. The impending event, while most emphatically future, is nevertheless operative in advance. With the emergence of Jesus, God is already at work, as he was at work in the preliminary victories of Cyrus, preparing to inaugurate his eschatological Reign. The signs of the coming Kingdom, concentrated in the person and activity of Jesus, are already there. Yet the decisive event itself has not yet taken place, any more than the return from exile had taken place at the time of the proclamation of Deutero-Isaiah. The Kingdom of God has not yet come, but it is near, so near that it is already operative in advance. This may not look, on the face of it, so very different from 'realized eschatology'. But there is in fact an all-important difference. 'Realized eschatology' asserts that the decisive event has already occurred. The view outlined here on the other hand seeks to give full, though not exaggerated, emphasis to what is already happening in the ministry of Jesus, yet at the same time to place the decisive event in the future.

(2) Matt. 12.28 = Luke 11.20: ἔφθασεν ἐφ᾽ ὑμᾶς ἡ βασιλεία τοῦ θεοῦ.

Dr. Dodd has argued[1] that ἔφθασεν here and ἤγγικεν in the passages just considered are alternative translations of the same Aramaic verb *mᵉṭa'* which means 'to reach', 'to arrive'. We have already seen that this meaning cannot be sustained with ἤγγικεν. Here, however, a much stronger case can be put up for the meaning 'to arrive'. To begin with, he has the support of Dalman[2] in postulating *mᵉṭa'* as the Aramaic

---

[1] *Parables*, pp. 44 f; E.T., XLVIII, pp. 138 ff.　　[2] *Worte Jesu*, p. 88.

original of ἔφθασεν here. Secondly, it is a fact that in Hellenistic Greek the verb φθάνω had largely lost its classical meaning of 'to anticipate' or 'to precede', and normally meant 'to arrive'. There are clear instances of this meaning at Rom. 9.31; II Cor. 10.14; Phil. 3.16; I Thess. 2.16. It could however on occasion retain its original classical sense. Moulton and Milligan[1] list nine examples from papyri, and there is a clear case of the classical meaning at I Thess. 4.15. In these cases however the context makes it clear that the notion of priority in the verb is to be retained. Elsewhere we must always assume that the Hellenistic sense of 'to arrive' is intended. Hence, in the passage under consideration the meaning is 'the kingdom of God has arrived upon you', exactly as Dr. Dodd maintains. This does not however necessarily imply a 'realized eschatology'. In I Thess. 2.16 we have the phrase ἔφθασε δὲ ἐπ' αὐτοὺς ἡ ὀργή. Here the use of ἡ ὀργή indicates that Paul is thinking of the eschatological wrath of God, which elsewhere he states is to come at the last day (Rom. 5.9; I Thess. 1.10). How comes it about that Paul speaks of an event as already happening which elsewhere he places unequivocally in the future? The answer is that he is using the familiar prophetic device of speaking of a future event as though it were already present. The certainty of the event is so overwhelming, the signs of its impendingness so sure, that it is said to have occurred, or to be occurring already.[2] Now it seems that we have a similar instance in the saying under consideration (Matt. 12.28 para.). The fact that the demons are yielding to his exorcisms is for Jesus so overwhelming proof, so vivid a sign, of the proximity of the Kingdom, that he speaks of it as though it had arrived already. There is a close parallel in Luke 10.18:

I beheld Satan fallen as lightning from heaven.

---

[1] *Vocabulary of the Greek New Testament* s.v.

[2] Cf. Davidson, *Hebrew Grammar*, [23]1930, p. 156: 'A lively imagination is very apt to conceive things which are really future, especially if their occurrence be certain, as already done, and to describe them in the perfect. . . . This usage is very common in the elevated language of the prophets, whose faith and imagination so vividly project them the event or scene which they predict that it appears already realized.' A. Oepke NT Deutsch *ad loc.* explains ἔφθασε in I Thess. 2.16 as a 'prophetic aorist'.

The context is the same—successful exorcisms, though here they are accomplished by the Seventy in the name of Jesus (verse 17). Their success is interpreted by Jesus as a sign of the approach of Satan's final overthrow at the End (cf. Rev. 12.9, etc.), which, with vivid prophetic imagination, he sees as an already accomplished fact. Hence Matt. 12.28 para., despite its *prima facie* meaning, actually supports our thesis that the Kingdom of God was for Jesus a future event.

(3) Mark 9.1.

Dr. Dodd[1] interprets thus: 'until they have seen that the Kingdom of God *has come* with power' (italics mine). The decisive argument against this interpretation is that ὁρᾶν is never used of intellectual perception.[2] Many commentators, faced with an apparently unfulfilled prediction, seek to evade the difficulty by referring the saying to some event other than the Parousia, e.g. the Transfiguration or the Fall of Jerusalem. The latest attempt in this direction is that of Dr. V. Taylor[3]: 'A visible manifestation of the rule of God in the life of the elect community.' All these interpretations overlook the plain sense of the words. The event referred to can only be the final coming of the Kingdom, as the words ἐν δυνάμει make abundantly clear. See e.g. Mark 13.26: 'And then shall they see the Son of man coming *with great power* and glory (μετὰ δυνάμεως).' Rom. 1.4: 'who was declared to be the Son of God *with power* (ἐν δυνάμει).' (In this passage the exaltation of Jesus after the Resurrection is interpreted as partially at least fulfilling the prediction of the Parousia.) I Cor. 15.43: 'it is sown in weakness: it is raised *in power* (ἐν δυνάμει).' Moreover Matthew referred Mark 9.1 to the future, for he has reworded the saying: 'till they see the Son of man coming in his kingdom' (Matt. 16.28). There can be no doubt that this is what Mark meant. The Parousia or coming of the Kingdom of God with power will take place in the lifetime of some (τινές), but not all of those present. Two further difficulties arise here. (i) We

[1] *Parables*, p. 42, pp. 53 f, cf. E.T. XLVIII, pp. 141 f.
[2] See the articles by Campbell and Creed in E.T. quoted above; Taylor, *Mark*, p. 385; Kümmel, *Verheissung*, pp. 19 ff.
[3] *Mark, ad loc.*

have here an unfulfilled prediction. (ii) In his indubitably authentic teaching Jesus consistently deprecated any attempt to fix the date of the End.[1] A suggestion has recently been made by G. Bornkamm[2] that Mark 9.1 is not a saying of the historical Jesus, but a prophetic 'word of the Lord' circulated in the early Church at a time when it was wrestling with the problems of a delayed Parousia.[3] He detects two further traces of such a word in the New Testament, viz., I Cor. 15.51 (introduced as a μυστήριον, a prophetic revelation) and I Thess. 4.15-17, explicitly ascribed to a 'word of the Lord'. It may be questioned however whether this is not too bold, and not really necessary, for the difficulties of Mark 9.1 are apparent rather than real. Jesus is not predicting the date of the Parousia, but assuring *some* of his followers that they will escape the martyrdom which he had foretold for others (Mark 8.34 f, etc.).[4] That the prediction of the Parousia was not fulfilled *in the way it was uttered* is not an insuperable difficulty. No doubt it was partially fulfilled in the exaltation of Jesus, and its final consummation delayed much longer than the prophetic foreshortening of the saying suggests.[5] But whatever the difficulties, there can be no doubt that it implies the coming of the Kingdom of God as a future event.

(4) Luke 17.21: ἡ βασιλεία τοῦ θεοῦ ἐντὸς ὑμῶν ἐστίν.

This saying, which occurs only in the special Lukan material, has been much discussed, and it is in fact a *crux interpretum*. It has been used to prove that Jesus held a purely inward, immanent conception of the Kingdom, or, alternatively, that while he accepted the transcendental conception, he is here asserting that the Kingdom is already present in the fullest sense. The meaning of ἐντὸς ὑμῶν cannot be decided: it may mean either 'within you' or 'among you'.[6] Any interpretation we give must leave open both possibilities. Now it is frequently overlooked that the point at issue in the context is

[1] Cf. Mark 13.32; Luke 17.24; Acts 1.7.
[2] *In Memoriam Ernst Lohmeyer*, 1951, pp. 116 ff.
[3] Cf. Bultmann, *Tradition*, p. 128.
[4] Cf. Jeremias, *Jesusworte*, p. 64.   [5] See below, p. 118 ff.
[6] See Dodd, *Parables*, p. 84; and Creed, *Luke*, *ad loc.*

not the nature of the Kingdom, but the question of the *signs of its advent*.[1] Jesus is concerned to repudiate the notion that the advent of the Kingdom is to be heralded by observable (μετὰ παρατηρήσεως) cosmic signs. The signs are of quite a different order: they are manifest in his own lowly mission and activity. Either then the coming Kingdom is operative 'within you' proleptically by its signs. That is to say, the signs of the coming Kingdom are to be sought in the hearts of men, in their response to the proclamation of Jesus. Or alternatively, the coming Kingdom is proleptically operative 'in your midst'—that is to say, Jesus himself, in his person as the bearer of the announcement of the dawning Kingdom, and in his healings and exorcisms, is the sign that the Kingdom of God is at hand. Whichever way we translate ἐντὸς ὑμῶν, the meaning of the saying is ultimately the same: the eschatological Kingdom is dawning, and the signs of its coming are already apparent in the presence and activity of Jesus—if only men had eyes to see and ears to hear.

There is another group of sayings in the primary documents which speak of 'entering' the Kingdom of God.

> Mark 9.47: And if thine eye cause thee to stumble, cast it out: it is good for thee to enter into the kingdom of God with one eye, rather than having two eyes to be cast into hell.

The phrase 'cast into hell' in the second half of the saying makes it quite clear that Jesus speaks here of future entry into the Kingdom when it comes at the End, not of a present possibility.

> Mark 10.23-25: How hardly shall they that have riches enter into the kingdom of God! . . . how hard is it for them that trust in riches to enter into the kingdom of God! It is easier for a camel to go through a needle's eye, than for a rich man to enter into the kingdom of God.

The use of the future (εἰσελεύσονται) in verse 23 makes it clear that the entry into the Kingdom of God in the two subsequent

[1] Cf. Dibelius, *Jesus*, 1949, p. 66.

verses is future, as in the previous instance, Mark 9.47: cf. also 10.15 (see below).

Matt. 7.21 (?Q): Not everyone that saith unto me, Lord, Lord, shall enter the kingdom of heaven.

The future εἰσελεύσεται and the reference to 'that day' (=the day of the Lord, the End) in verse 22 make it abundantly clear that Jesus is thinking here of the Kingdom of God as a future event, and we may safely conclude that all the 'entry' sayings imply this.

Another word employed is 'seek' (ζητεῖν), e.g. in Matt. 6.33 para.: 'Seek ye first his kingdom'. This saying might imply that the Kingdom to be sought for is a present reality. But it could equally be an appeal to orientate one's present behaviour towards a future event. And in view of the future orientation of the Sermon on the Mount as a whole[1] the second alternative is preferable.

A third word is 'received' (δέχεσθαι).

Mark 10.15: Whosoever shall not receive the kingdom of God as a little child, he shall in no wise enter therein.

The second half of the saying is an 'entry' logion, therefore the first part must also be referred to a future event. 'Receive' means 'receive, not the kingdom of God as a present reality, but the present *proclamation* of the future event'—just as in the phrase 'receive the word of God' (Acts 8.14, etc.). It is men's acceptance of Jesus' proclamation of the coming Kingdom which decides their entry or rejection when it comes. Cf. Mark 8.38; Luke 12.8 (Q).

Other passages speak of the qualifications for future entry:

Mark 10.14: Of such (viz., the childlike) is the kingdom of God.

Coming as it does immediately before verse 15, which excludes future entry to the unchildlike, this verse is the corresponding promise. The Kingdom is 'theirs', not in the sense that they already possess it as a present reality, but in the sense that they have the certainty of the promise. The childlike are those who

---

[1] Cf. the Beatitudes, see below.

accept Jesus' proclamation of the coming Kingdom with humble faith.

> Mark 12.34: Thou art not far from the kingdom of God.

As in the previous instance, Jesus is speaking of the right disposition for future entry. The scribe in the context was almost on the brink of accepting the proclamation of Jesus, and therefore Jesus can say to him—almost, but not quite, for the decision has not been clinched—'Yours is the Kingdom of God.'[1]

> Matt. 5.3. para.: For theirs is the kingdom of heaven (cf. verse 10).

The future tenses attached to all the other Beatitudes (shall be comforted, shall inherit the earth, shall be filled, shall obtain mercy, shall see God) make it quite clear that we have here, as in the two Markan passages just considered, a promise of future entry into the Kingdom when it comes.

There is a very difficult saying which appears in different forms in Matthew and Luke, but which obviously represents varying traditions of the same logion:

Matt. 11.12-13*a*	Luke 16.16
And from the days of John the Baptist until now the kingdom of heaven suffereth violence, and men of violence take it by force. For all the prophets and the law prophesied until John.	The law and the prophets were until John: from that time the gospel of the kingdom of God is preached, and every man entereth violently into it.

It is generally held, with good reason, that Matthew gives us the more original form of the saying. Luke has transformed what was to him an enigmatic saying and made it expressive of his missionary and universalist motif.[2] We will therefore consider the Matthean form. It is clear that John the Baptist marks the dividing point between two epochs, the first characterized by the law and the prophets, the second in some sense

---

[1] Cf. Rawlinson, *Mark*; Blunt, *Mark, ad loc.*
[2] Cf. Creed, *Luke, ad loc.*; and Schrenk, T.W.N.T., I, pp. 608 ff.

by the Kingdom of God.[1] It would be possible[2] to take βιάζεται (which R.V. takes as passive: 'suffereth violence') as a middle, 'exercising its force' (so Otto). Even if this be the correct interpretation, there is no need to follow Dr. Dodd in supposing this to mean that with Jesus the Kingdom had already come. It need mean no more than that the proclamation of the coming Kingdom is taking place, that the signs of its impending advent are being performed by Jesus, and that in this proleptic sense the Kingdom, though not having come, is 'exercising its force', i.e. is operative in advance. That at any rate seems to be the way Luke understood it, for he paraphrases βιάζεται by εὐαγγιλίζεται. But this interpretation of βιάζεται as a middle seems to be ruled out by the following clause, which explains that the violence in question is not the action of the Kingdom, but of violent men (βιασταί). Hence R.V. is probably right in taking βιάζεται as a passive. How then does the Kingdom 'suffer violence'? Probably in the resistance encountered by its proclamation. The advantage of this interpretation is that it brings the saying into line with the following parable of the Children in the Market Place, which is also concerned with the resistance of Israel to the proclamation of the Kingdom. The second clause of our saying will then mean that the violent men, who resist the message of Jesus, are also preventing others from accepting the message. They snatch away (ἁρπάζουσιν, cf. Matt. 13.19) the word from the hearers, and prevent them from entering into the sphere of the eschatological salvation (cf. Matt. 23.13). Whichever way therefore we interpret this difficult saying, it does not necessarily imply a realized eschatology, any more than the earlier sayings. The Reign of God is already breaking in proleptically in the proclamation and signs of Jesus (that is the difference between the time of Jesus's ministry and the time of John the Baptist), but it would be to overstate the case to say that with Jesus the Kingdom of God has actually come.

Matthew links the foregoing logion very closely with another saying from the Q material:

[1] Cf. Dodd, *Parables*, p. 48.
[2] Cf. Otto, *Kingdom*, p. 108.

Matt. 11.11 para.: He that is but little in the kingdom of heaven is greater than he (sc. John the Baptist).

Once more, this saying must not be pressed to imply that the Kingdom of God has already come. It is really a saying which belongs to the group of 'qualification' sayings (see above). It refers to the same people of whom the beatitudes assert that 'theirs is the Kingdom of heaven'.

The numerous instances where the Kingdom of God is spoken of in connexion with the parables will be dealt with in the following section.

There are four other passages whose future reference even the most ardent champion of realized eschatology can hardly deny, viz., Mark 14.25: 'Verily I say unto you, I will no more drink of the fruit of the vine, until that day when I drink it new in the kingdom of God'; Matt. 8.11 para.: 'Many shall come from the east and the west, and shall sit down . . . in the kingdom of heaven'; Matt. 6.10 para.: 'Thy kingdom come.' Then there is the important saying at Luke 12.32 ('Fear not, little flock; for it is your Father's good pleasure to give you the kingdom'), which, though attested only by the special Lukan material, has a high claim to authenticity.[1] The attempt of Dr. Dodd to explain away the obvious future reference of these sayings,[2] especially when he relegates Mark 14.25 to 'the transcendent order beyond space and time' (a wholly non-biblical, Platonic conception!) is singularly unconvincing. No amount of explaining away can alter the fact that in all four sayings Jesus quite unequivocally speaks of the coming of the Kingdom of God as a future event, which, however imminent it may be, however proleptically active here and now in his ministry, is nevertheless an event which has not itself yet taken place, but which still lies in the future.

Finally, there are some sayings which, though they do not explicitly mention the Kingdom of God, are adduced in support of the thesis of realized eschatalogy[3]:

Matt. 13.16-17 para.: Blessed are your eyes, for they see;

---

[1] Despite its rejection by Bultmann in *Tradition*, p. 116, p. 134.
[2] *Parables*, pp. 53 ff.   [3] See Dodd, *Parables*, pp. 46 f.

and your ears, for they hear. For verily I say unto you, that many prophets and righteous men desired to see the things which ye see, and saw them not; and to hear the things which ye hear, and heard them not.

The best commentary on this saying is provided by the Reply to John in Matt. 11.2-6 para., where the same verbs 'hear' and 'see' (ἀκούειν and βλέπειν) recur, and where the 'things seen' are defined as the healings performed by Jesus (the blind receive their sight, etc.) and the 'things heard' as his proclamation (the poor have good tidings preached to them). The healings, as we shall see later, are signs pointing forward to the imminent future event of the coming of the Kingdom, and the proclamation, as we have already seen, is the proclamation of the coming Kingdom.[1] So in Matt. 13.16 f the disciples (verse 10) are pronounced blessed, because they, unlike the prophets and righteous men of old, who looked forward to the Kingdom from afar, are privileged to see and hear the signs of the coming Kingdom in the ministry of Jesus, and thus to witness, not its arrival, but its dawning.

Matt. 12.41-42 para.: The men of Nineveh shall stand up in the judgement with this generation, and shall condemn it: for they repented at the preaching of Jonah; and behold, a greater than Jonah is here. The queen of the south shall rise up in the judgement with this generation, and shall condemn it: for she came from the ends of the earth to hear the wisdom of Solomon; and behold, a greater than Solomon is here.

Dr. Dodd has rightly pointed out[2] that the 'greater' in these two verses is neuter (πλεῖον) not masculine, and should therefore be translated '*something* greater'. But what is that 'something greater'? Surely, what is contrasted is the reaction of the Ninevites to the preaching (κήρυγμα, verse 41) of Jonah with the reaction of this generation to the preaching of Jesus, viz., his proclamation that the Kingdom of heaven is at their doors. The 'something greater' is the proclamation of Jesus

[1] See also the discussion of the verb εὐαγγελίζεται below, p. 36.
[2] *Parables*, p. 46, footnote 1.

Similarly in the next verse the proclamation of Jesus is 'something greater' than the wisdom of Solomon. In neither case is the πλεῖον the already realized Kingdom.

2. THE SIGNS OF THE COMING KINGDOM

It has become fashionable to interpret the miracles of Jesus as signs of a realized eschatology, as signs that with the appearance of Jesus the Kingdom of God had already come, and that in them he is already acting as Messiah.[1]

There are two passages, both in Q, which are crucial for our Lord's understanding of his own miracles, the Reply to John in Prison and the Beelzebul controversy.

(i) *The Reply to John*, Matt. 11.2-6 = Luke 7.18-22

We set out here the crucial words in Greek in one column, and two passages from the LXX of Isaiah in the other:

τυφλοὶ ἀναβλέπουσι,	τότε ἀνοιχθήσονται ὀφθαλμοὶ τυφλῶν,
καὶ χωλοὶ περιπατοῦσι·	καὶ ὦτα κωφῶν ἀκούσονται. τότε
(λεπροὶ καθαρίζονται),	ἁλεῖται ὡς ἔλαφος ὁ χωλός....
καὶ κωφοὶ ἀκούουσι·	(Isa. 35.5-6)
καὶ νεκροὶ ἐγείρονται,	εὐαγγελίσασθαι πτωχοῖς (Isa. 61.1)
καὶ πτωχοὶ εὐαγγελίζονται.	

That we have here reminiscences of Isa. 35 and 61 has frequently been noted.[2] It is worth observing, however, as the above columns make clear, that there is no *direct* quotation of either of these passages. There can be no question therefore of the Hellenistic Churches having deliberately combined two

---

[1] See e.g. Richardson, *Miracles*, pp. 38 ff. Professor Richardson is not however always consistent. On p. 38 he writes: 'If we examine the utterances attributed to Jesus himself in the Synoptic Gospels on the subject of his own miracles, we find that he regarded them as evidences of the *drawing nigh* of the Kingdom of God.' Yet in a footnote on the same page he quotes with approval Dr. Dodd's statement in his *Parables* that the phrase ἔφθασεν ἐφ' ἡμᾶς ἡ βασιλεία τοῦ θεοῦ 'expresses in the most vivid and forceful way the fact that the Kingdom of God has *actually arrived*'. Again, on p. 43, where Professor Richardson discusses the Q logion Matt. 11.4 f para., he writes 'there can be no doubt that they (viz., this logion) are intended to assert that the Messianic age of the Isaianic prediction *had already arrived*' (italics mine). It is difficult to harmonize 'drawing nigh' with 'already arrived' but on balance Professor Richardson clearly favours the latter.

[2] Cf. Richardson. *Miracles*, p. 43 and p. 83.

35

quotations from the LXX and placed them into the mouth of Jesus. They are rather the product of a mind which has soaked itself in the message of Isaiah as a whole, a circumstance which gives the saying a high claim to authenticity. Now Isa. 35 presents the Messianic salvation as a process. First, there is the journey through the wilderness, to facilitate which the miraculous healings of verses 5 and 6 are provided. Then, as the decisive, culminating event as the fulfilment of the Messianic salvation, comes the return to Zion in verse 10. The miraculous healings therefore are not so much signs that the Messianic age 'has dawned', as signs that it 'is dawning'. The distinction may seem subtle, and somewhat over-drawn, but nevertheless it is of great importance when applied to the miracles of Jesus. For, in applying Isa. 35 to his own works of healing, and claiming, not that the age of salvation has already come, but rather that it 'is dawning', Jesus places the decisive event, the fulfilment of the Messianic salvation, in the future. Again, the key word in the allusion to Isa. 61 is εὐαγγελίζονται, itself a key word in the prophecies of the earlier chapters which we now know as Deutero-Isaiah (40-55), but which Jesus of course would have attributed to the same author as Isa. 61:

O thou *that tellest good tidings*[1] to Zion,
    get thee up into the high mountain;
O thou that *tellest good tidings*[1] to Jerusalem,
    lift up thy voice with strength (Isa. 40.9).

I will give to Jerusalem *one that bringeth good tidings*[2]
(Isa. 41.27).

How beautiful upon the mountains are the feet of him *that bringeth good tidings*,[3] that publisheth peace, that *bringeth good tidings* of good,[3] that publisheth salvation; that saith unto Zion, Thy God reigneth! (Isa. 52.7).

Let us recall once more[4] the situation in which the unknown prophet is speaking. The return from exile has not yet taken

[1] ὁ εὐαγγελιζόμενος, Mᵉbhǎssĕrĕth.
[2] Mᵉbhǎssēr; LXX has a different reading.
[3] εὐαγγελιζομένου mᵉbhǎssēr.   [4] Cf. p. 25.

place, but things are in motion. Cyrus is already winning his preliminary victories. God is already at work, and the decisive event is just round the corner. Hence the verb εὐαγγελίζονται in the answer to John must not be evacuated of its future reference. The proclamation of Jesus is part of the initial stages of the End, but the End itself has not yet occurred. That is the meaning of the answer to John. With the healings and the proclamation of Jesus the new age is dawning, but it has not yet arrived. The decisive event still lies in the future.

(ii) *The Beelzebul Controversy* (Luke 11.17-22 para.)

The crucial saying in this *pericope* is:

> If I by the finger (Matthew: Spirit) of God cast out devils, then is the kingdom of God come upon you (Luke 11.20).

There is general agreement that the Lukan version of the saying is more primitive than the Matthean[1] and that 'finger of God' is an allusion to Ex. 8.19 (Heb. and LXX: verse 15).[2] Now this allusion to Ex. 8.15 (19) may have a deeper significance than is usually recognized. For the plagues of Egypt, wrought by the *finger* of God, were preliminary demonstrations of power pointing forward to the decisive act of God, the Exodus itself, which at Ex. 15.6 is attributed to the *right hand* of God. The plagues of Egypt, that is to say, were not themselves the great event, but signs wrought by God as pointers to the accomplishment of the great event in the near future. Now I suggest that by ascribing his exorcisms to the finger of God Jesus is placing them in the same relation to his own Exodus, which during his ministry still lies in the future,[3] as the plagues of Egypt bore to the original Exodus, which contemporary Jewish thought regarded as a type of the eschatological redemption.[4] In view of this widely accepted typology,

---

[1] Cf. Richardson, *Miracles*, p. 39; T. W. Manson, *Teaching*, pp. 82 f; Barrett, *Spirit*, pp. 62 f.

[2] Professor T. W. Manson (*ibid.*) states, though without offering any reason, that the phrase 'finger of God' is derived from the Hebrew, but so far as the language is concerned, it could equally be a reminiscence of the LXX (δάκτυλος θεοῦ).

[3] Cf. Luke 9.31, and the paschal background of the Last Supper.

[4] Cf. Jeremias, *Kindertaufe*, pp. 16 f and especially 1 Cor. 10.1-13.

it does not seem too far fetched to suggest that it was present to the mind of Jesus when he used the phrase 'finger of God'. At all events, the same preliminary character of the exorcisms is brought out in the Markan version of the Beelzebul controversy, which is independent of that in Q, and which omits the saying about the finger of God:

> But no one can enter into the house of the strong man, and spoil his goods, except he first bind the strong man; and then he will spoil his house (Mark 3.27).

The exorcisms of Jesus are the preliminary assault on the kingdom of Satan, preparatory to his final overthrow at the End. The strong man must *first* ($\pi\rho\hat{\omega}\tau o\nu$) be bound, and then ($\tau\acute{o}\tau\epsilon$) his goods can be spoiled. The $\pi\rho\hat{\omega}\tau o\nu$ refers to the ministry of Jesus, the $\tau\acute{o}\tau\epsilon$ to the decisive event of the future.

In tracing the interpretation of the miracles of Jesus to a background provided by the 'signs' wrought by Moses before the Exodus, and to the 'signs' foretold by Deutero-Isaiah as preceding the eschatological return to Zion, we have implied that the miracles of Jesus were also 'signs'. As a matter of fact, however, Jesus never applies the word 'sign' to his miraculous activity. On the contrary, according to both Mark and Q, he uses the word 'sign' in a depreciating sense. According to Mark Jesus refused point blank to give any 'sign' to the Pharisees when they demanded 'a sign from heaven':

> Why doth this generation seek a sign? Verily I say unto you, There shall no sign be given unto this generation (Mark 8.12).

It is difficult to determine in what sense a sign is demanded and in what sense it is refused. Some critics take the sign in question to mean a supernatural cosmological phenomenon such as Jewish Apocalyptic believed would precede the End, and of which, according to the Little Apocalypse, Jesus himself is alleged to have spoken in Mark 13.24 ff para. Others[1] interpret the sign demanded as an action authenticating the *present* claims of Jesus. Now it is worth noting that in asking their

[1] e.g. Taylor, *Mark*, *ad loc.*

question the Pharisees are said to be *tempting* Jesus (πειράζοντες, verse 11). The use of this verb recalls the temptation of Jesus by the devil in its Q form (Matt. 4.3 ff para.), where the purpose of the temptation is to make Jesus use his miraculous powers to point *to himself*. This is just what the Pharisees are demanding in Mark 8.11. Like the devil in the Temptation,[1] they tempt Jesus to perform some striking act to prove who he is. Jesus rejects this kind of sign *in toto*. It is, as Mark rightly insists, a temptation. If this is what is meant by a sign, then no sign shall be given to this generation. Jesus refuses, not to perform signs as such, but signs intended to point to *himself*. Thus the miracles of Jesus were not intended to be, and must not be interpreted as, signs that he was the Messiah.[2] The best commentary on the refusal of Jesus to give any sign as a proof of Messiahship is furnished by the Christological hymn in Phil. 2.6:

> Who, being in the form of God, counted it not a thing to be grasped (R.V. marg. = ἁρπαγμόν) to be on an equality with God . . . becoming obedient.

Had Jesus performed signs as a proof of his Messiahship, he would have been treating the Messiahship precisely as an ἁρπαγμός, a thing to be grasped at. Hence his absolute refusal to give the kind of sign the Pharisees require. Their request is a diabolical temptation, and he rejects it with an oath: ἀμὴν λέγω ὑμῖν εἰ (Heb. *'im*) δοθήσεται. . . .[3] While, then, Jesus' absolute refusal to give a sign in Mark 8.11 is no proof that Jesus did not regard his miracles as signs pointing forward to the coming eschatological Kingdom it does appear to prove conclusively that he refused to interpret them as signs of an already exercised Messiahship.

In the Q version, this refusal to give a sign is qualified:

> An evil and adulterous generation seeketh after a sign; and there shall no sign be given to it but the sign of Jonah the prophet. (Matt. 12.39 para.; cf. Matt. 16.4, where

---

[1] The historicity of the Q version of the Temptation is discussed below, p. 84.
[2] The question of the Messiahship of Jesus is discussed below in Chapter IV.
[3] For the oath form cf. LXX Ps. 94.11 (Heb. and Eng. Ps. 95.11), cited at Heb. 3.11, 4.3, 5.

Matthew has inserted the qualification from Q into his Markan source.)

There is no need to accept the suggestion[1] that 'Jonah' is a corruption for 'John' (= John the Baptist). Nor can we agree with the judgement of Mr. C. K. Barrett[2] that Matthew's interpretation (12.40) of the sign of Jonah as a reference to the death and Resurrection of Jesus is what Jesus himself intended. For in the continuation of the passage in Q Jonah is adduced as a parallel to Jesus and his activity in respect of his *kerygma* (Matt. 12.41 para.).[3] Here, then, in the word *kerygma* we have a clue to Jesus' meaning. The only sign of the coming Kingdom given will be his own proclamation of the imminent advent of the Kingdom. This concession in Q is not incompatible with the absolute refusal in Mark, for the sign conceded is of a wholly different order from the sign demanded. The sign demanded was a sign vindicating the personal authority of Jesus; the sign conceded is a sign pointing forward to the coming Kingdom. That sign is to be sought exclusively in the kerygmatic activity of Jesus. But the miracles of Jesus are part and parcel of his kerygmatic activity. This is implied in the Reply to John, where the preaching of the gospel to the poor is bracketed with the healings as signs of the coming Kingdom,[4] and in the Beelzebul controversy, where the exorcisms are made to convey the same message as the proclamation: 'the Kingdom of God has come upon you.' In fact the miracles are part of the proclamation itself, quite as much as spoken words of Jesus. A similar view is presented at Mark 6.5, where it is stated that Jesus limited his miraculous activity in Nazareth because its inhabitants rejected his *kerygma* (they refused to accept him as a 'prophet,' verse 4). Mark states bluntly that he 'could' (ἐδύνατο) do no act of power there. Why this startling admission of inability? Surely, because such acts of power *apart from their subordination to the kerygma*, would be outside the scope of his mission. Detached from the *kerygma*, they become independent displays

---

[1] J. H. Michael, J.T.S., XXI, pp. 146-159.   [2] *Spirit*, p. 90.
[3] See above, p. 34.   [4] See above, p. 35 f.

of power, which call men's attention to himself and away from the coming Kingdom. As such, they would be a diabolical temptation. That Jesus therefore consented to give only one sign, the sign of the prophet Jonah, does not mean that he did not regard his miracles as signs. They were themselves part of the 'sign of the prophet Jonah', for they were a part of Jesus' own proclamation.

The story of the Paralytic (Mark 2.1-12) raises a number of problems. It is the only miracle where a physical healing is brought into direct connexion with the proclamation of forgiveness of sins. This circumstance and difficulties of style and form have led many critics to conclude that the connexion between the declaration of forgiveness and the physical healing is the work of the evangelist.[1] Mark, it is held, has inserted a controversial dialogue into the bosom of a simple story of healing. It would be an easy way out of a difficulty if we could deal with the controversial dialogue in this way. We could then regard it as a product of *Gemeindetheologie*, and would have no need to take it into account in reconstructing the interpretation which Jesus placed upon his miracles. On the other hand it is by no means certain that the connexion between the miracles and forgiveness of sin is as unique as would appear at first sight. In Mark 5.34 para. and Mark 10.52 para. Jesus says to one whom he has healed: ἡ πίστις σου σέσωκέ σε.[2] The verb σώζω could of course refer merely to the physical healing, but its use in Luke 7.50 after verse 48 ('Thy sins are forgiven') shows that there at any rate it is synonymous with the forgiving of sins. It is therefore quite possible that we are meant to take the verb σώζω, when used in connexion with the healings, in this wider sense. This will mean that the evangelists certainly, and the Lord himself quite probably, connected the miracles with the eschatological salvation. But in what way were the two things connected? Did Jesus already in his earthly ministry dispense the eschatological salvation? No doubt the evangelists, who knew him as the Lord of the Church, dispensing the

---

[1] See Taylor, *Mark, ad loc., Tradition*, pp. 66-8; Bultmann, *Tradition*, pp. 12-14, p. 227; Rawlinson, *Mark, ad loc.*
[2] Cf. Luke 7.50, 17.19, special Lukan material.

eschatological salvation through word and sacrament, interpreted the miracles and pronouncements of Jesus in this sense. But in view of Jesus' basic proclamation of the Kingdom as on its way, but still decisively to come, it is difficult to suppose that historically he could have claimed so much. Rather, we must interpret ἄφεσις and σωτηρία in that same proleptic sense in which we interpreted ἔφθασεν ἐφ' ὑμᾶς ἡ βασιλεία at Luke 11.20.[1] The ἄφεσις and σωτηρία dispensed to individuals in the course of Jesus' ministry are instalments in advance made available as signs of what will later become universally available through the decisive event of the coming of the Kingdom. As Hoskyns and Davey write in commenting on this episode[2]: 'The physical miracles are external signs of the supreme messianic miracle, the rescue of men from the grip of the powers of evil—from sin. The supreme messianic miracle to which the miracles point is the salvation of men by the power of the living God exercised through the agency of the messiah.' But, in the perspective of the gospels, and as we shall hope to show in the next chapter in the perspective of Jesus himself, the supreme Messianic miracle is accomplished on the cross. Moreover, Mark himself hints at this future reference of the Healing of the Paralytic to the cross by his suggestion that this Jesus who heals the man and conveys to him forgiveness is the One who is even now on the way to the cross, already encountering the same opposition of his enemies (verses 6 and 7), and already incurring the same charge of 'blasphemy' (verse 7), which are to bring him to the cross (Mark 14.64). Mark intends his readers to see in this miracle the crucified and exalted Lord dispensing in advance the fruits of his passion which they know he dispenses in the life of the Church in virtue of his death and Resurrection.[3]

Before leaving the subject of the miracles of Jesus, let us glance briefly at the Johannine interpretation of the signs as

[1] See above, p. 25 f.
[2] *Riddle*, p. 120.
[3] A further passage which brings out the preliminary character of Jesus' miracles is the Matthean version of the Gadarene Demoniac: ἦλθες ὧδε πρὸ καιροῦ βασανίσαι ἡμᾶς; Matt. 8.29. This passage is omitted in the above discussion, however, because the crucial phrase πρὸ καιροῦ is a Matthean addition to Mark.

indicated by the first sign in John 2.1-11, the changing of the water into wine at Cana of Galilee. The clue to the interpretation of this sign lies in verse 4*b*: 'mine hour is not yet come' and in verse 6: 'after the Jews' manner of purifying'.[1] The episode points forward to the 'hour' (12.23; 13.1; 17.1) of the glorification of Jesus on the cross, when the eschatological purification from sin (John 19.34; cf. 1 John 1.7) will be accomplished. *'Until that time* his actions are signs of *what is to be.'*[2] Although in 2.11 John says that in this miracle Jesus 'manifested forth his glory', he does not mean us to understand that the miracle is an independent manifestation of the Messianic glory. It is a glimpse in advance of that 'glory' which will be finally and decisively manifested in the death and exaltation of Jesus. Here also lies the clue to the enigmatic saying in John 14.12:

> Verily, verily, I say unto you, He that believeth on me, the works that I do shall he do also; and greater works than these shall he do; because I go unto the Father.

The works which Jesus did in his earthly ministry were signs pointing forward to the work he will accomplish by going to the Father. The works which those who believe on him, i.e. his Church, will do then, namely the preaching of the word and the administration of the sacraments, will be, like the works of Jesus' ministry, signs, but they will be greater works. For in the meantime by going to the Father Jesus will have accomplished the decisive Messianic work, and the Spirit, which during the Lord's earthly ministry was not yet given, because he was not yet glorified (7.39) will have been released (20.22). Therefore the works of the Church, its proclamation and its sacraments, will not, like the miracles, point forward as preliminary instalments to the Messianic salvation, they will actually mediate it, and in this sense they will be 'greater works' than those which Jesus wrought during his ministry.

[1] Cf. Hoskyns and Davey, *The Fourth Gospel*, 1940, *ad loc.*; O. Cullmann, *Urchristentum und Gottesdienst*, 1950, pp. 67 ff; Eng. Trans. *Early Christian Worship*, 1952, pp. 66 ff.
[2] Hoskyns, *loc. cit.*, italics mine

3. THE PARABLES OF THE COMING KINGDOM

It is the main thesis of Dr. Dodd's *Parables* that the parables imply a 'realized eschatology' already in the ministry of Jesus. We propose therefore to examine a selection of the parables in order to show this that is not necessarily so.

(i) *The Sower* (Mark 4.3-8 para.)

Assuming with most modern critics[1] that the allegorical interpretation given in Mark 4.13-20 para. is secondary, we may consider the parable on its own merits. The point of it lies in the contrast between the wastage during the sowing, and the abundant harvest which despite the wastage is eventually secured. It was probably told in view of some concrete situation in the ministry of Jesus which we can no longer recover, but which we may reasonably infer was a situation of apparent failure.[2] Now the harvest is a biblical image for the End.[3] A situation of failure is thus brought into relation with the coming End. Failure, so far from ruling out the coming of the End, is precisely the cost of its achievement. The failure of the proclamation will culminate in the failure of the cross, but out of it will come the triumphant conclusion of the End. Perhaps the Fourth Evangelist has given us precisely this interpretation of the parable of the Sower in summary form in the words: 'Except a grain of wheat fall into the earth and die, it abideth by itself alone; but if it die, it beareth much fruit' (John 12.24). However that may be, the parable quite clearly implies that the End is still to come.

(ii) *The Seed Growing Secretly.* (Mark 4.26-29; no parallel in Matthew or Luke)

This parable depicts God's plan of salvation as involving first a period of secret growth, and then the decisive event of the End. Dr. Dodd has urged[4] that the period of growth

---

[1] e.g. Dodd, *Parables*, pp. 180 ff; Taylor, *Mark, ad loc.*; J. Jeremias, *The Parables of Jesus*, pp. 61 ff.

[2] Failure in the ministry of Jesus is indicated at Mark 6.1-6 (Nazareth); Matt. 11.21 para. (Chorazin and Bethsaida); these instances might provide a 'life situation' for the parable of the Sower.

[3] See the quotations in Hoskyns and Davey, *Riddle*, pp. 130 f; and cf. Dodd, *Parables*, p. 178.   [4] *Parables*, pp. 179 f.

represents the 'long history of God's dealings with his people' and the harvest the ministry of Jesus. But, we might ask, does a period of secret growth readily suggest the Old Testament salvation history? Were the Exodus or the mission of the prophets obscure? Surely, it is more natural to identify the period of secret growth with the ministry of Jesus. In that case the End, as in the parable of the Sower, is yet to come. On this interpretation the purpose of the parable becomes clear. It is meant to warn the disciples not to try and take matters into their own hands. They may think that the movement Jesus has inaugurated is not getting them anywhere, and that they must therefore, like the Zealots (was it perhaps addressed particularly to Simon the Zealot or to Judas Iscariot?), do something drastic, and so hasten the coming of the Kingdom for themselves? No—they must wait patiently like the husbandman for the divine intervention. The parable, on this interpretation, contains a warning and an encouragement which it lacks on Dr. Dodd's interpretation. The implication is that while the initial stages of the coming of the Kingdom are already at work (the growing of the seed) in the obscure activity of Jesus, the decisive event of its coming still lies in the future.

(iii) *The Mustard Seed and the Leaven* (Mark 4.30 para.; Matt. 13.33 para.)

The point of these twin parables is that obscure beginnings do not rule out ultimate success. The ministry of Jesus is a very obscure beginning for the supreme cosmic event of the End, but that does not invalidate the claim that it is a sign of the coming Kingdom. Yet the humble beginnings are organically related to the future event. God is already initiating in the ministry of Jesus a movement which will issue in the coming of the End.

(iv) *The Fig Tree* (Mark 13.28-29 para.)

The attempt of Dr. Dodd and others to read a 'realized eschatalogy' into this parable[1] is singularly unconvincing. As

---

[1] Dodd, *Parables*, p. 137; Smith, *Parables*, 1937, pp. 89 ff (apparently, though his interpretation is obscure); Taylor, *Mark, ad loc.*

the leaves of the fig tree are the signs, not that summer has arrived, but that it is close at hand (ἐγγύς), so the ministry of Jesus is a sign of the approaching Kingdom. The Kingdom, like the summer, is still a future event, but things are already happening: the signs of the coming End are already there.

(v) *The Cloud and the South Wind* (Luke 12.54-56; cf. Matt. 16.2-3)

With the parable of the Fig Tree we may aptly compare these little parabolic sayings, recorded in rather different forms in Matthew and Luke:

> When ye see a cloud rising in the west, straightway ye say, There cometh a shower; and so it cometh to pass. And when ye see a south wind blowing, ye say, There will be a scorching heat; and it cometh to pass. Ye hypocrites, ye know how to interpret the face of the earth and the heaven; but how is it that ye know not how to interpret this time? (Matt.: 'the signs of the times').

Here is another lucid expression of the relation between Jesus' ministry on the one hand and the coming Kingdom on the other. The cloud has appeared in the sky, the shower is imminent; the south wind rising, the scorching heat will arrive at any moment. But like the shower and the scorching heat, the decisive event of the End is still future. If the multitude had eyes to see and ears to hear, they would discern the *kairoi* of redemption history as surely as they can produce a weather forecast. But it requires the insight of faith to discern in Jesus and his activity the signs of the coming Kingdom.

(vi) *Agree with thine Adversary* (Luke 12.58-59; cf. Matt. 5.25-26)

Luke follows up these little parabolic sayings with a saying which in Matthew (5.25) has been transformed into a community rule, but which was undoubtedly in its original form a parable:

> For as thou art going with thine adversary before the magistrate, on the way give diligence to be quit of him; lest haply he hale thee unto the judge, and the judge shall deliver thee to the officer, and the officer shall cast thee into prison.

The point of this little parable is the necessity of decision while there is yet time. Once more the situation presupposed is the same. The ministry of Jesus, with its proclamation of the imminent advent of God's Reign, is a brief interval which God is allowing Israel for decision (cf. the Barren Fig Tree in its Lukan form as a parable, Luke 13.6-9).

(vii) *Parables of Decision*

Other parables also call for a decision in face of an event, not which has already happened, but which is impending. Such is the point of the Ten Virgins (Matt. 25.1-13), the Rich Fool (Luke 12.16-20), and the twin parables of the Pearl and the Hidden Treasure (Matt. 13.44-46), which speak of sacrificing everything (i.e. making a radical decision) in view of a prize set before one (i.e. the coming Kingdom).

(viii) *Parables of Rejection*

Lastly, a number of parables are concerned with the rejection by Israel of Jesus' proclamation of the imminent advent of the Kingdom. The parable of the Money in Trust (Matt. 25.14-30 and Luke 19.12-27) warns the hearers of a judgement which is impending on those who reject the proclamation. The situation presupposed by the parable of the Marriage Feast (Matt. 22.2-14; Luke 14.16-24) is that the ministry of Jesus is the period during which the invitations are being sent out. The righteous in Israel, those who were bidden, are refusing the invitation, and so it is being re-addressed to the '*am ha-'areç*, the publicans and sinners. But the banquet, though ready (ἕτοιμα, Luke 14.17), has not started. So the banquet of the Kingdom is still future (cf. the future φάγεται in verse 15).

Finally there is the parable of the Vineyard (Mark 12.1-9 para.). Like the parable of the Great Supper or Marriage Feast, it implies that 'all things are now ready'. The history of redemption is rapidly drawing to its climax. The culmination of that history is the sending of the Son. The Son ought not to be allegorized and treated as a public claim of Jesus to be the Messiah, but it does mean that in his proclamation of the

47

Kingdom with its accompanying signs the history of redemption is reaching its climax. These signs the Jewish authorities are rejecting—this is the point reached at the moment of narration. Then comes the question about the future: What then will the Lord of the Vineyard do? The answer given is that the eschatological judgement will be pronounced over Israel: when the Kingdom comes they will be excluded and others will enter. Once again, the decisive event lies neither in the present, nor in the past, but in the very near future.

The situation implied by the parables therefore, is exactly that implied by Jesus' own interpretation of his miracles. The Kingdom of God is not yet present, it is imminent; but the imminent event is already at work, producing the signs of its coming. The Kingdom is dawning, but it has not yet arrived.

4. THE IMPORTANCE OF NON-REALIZED ESCHATOLOGY

The reader may perhaps have the impression that the interpretation of the eschatological proclamation of Jesus adumbrated in the foregoing pages is not after all so very far removed from the 'realized eschatology' which has borne the brunt of our criticism. For we have conceded that something was already happening in the ministry of Jesus, that God was already acting in his proclamation, works of power and teaching, that these activities were organically related to the End as the growing of the seed is organically related to the harvest, and that in some sense they might be described as proleptic instalments of the final blessings of the End. Is not this very close to what Dr. Dodd is after all contending for in his *Parables*? Such an impression would be erroneous. Realized eschatology asserts that the Kingdom 'has come'. It asserts that the decisive event has already taken place, at the Baptism of Jesus, at his birth at Bethlehem perhaps, or at the moment of the Incarnation. Any surviving traces of futurist eschatology would at best be the dotting of the i's and the crossing of the t's of what had already happened, or at the lowest estimate an 'accommodation of language'. But to place the decisive event in the past or present in this way not only does violence to the texts in which Jesus speaks of the Kingdom of God, not only fails to do justice to the way in which our Lord's earthly ministry is keyed up to a future event, to the tension which manifests itself on every page of the gospels, but, above all, *it destroys*—as we shall see in the following chapter—*the cruciality of the cross.*

III

THE KINGDOM OF
GOD AND THE DEATH
OF JESUS

AT this point it will be useful to remind ourselves of Bultmann's interpretation of Jesus. It is, that Jesus was an eschatological prophet who announced the impending advent of the Reign of God, and his own person and activity as the signs of its coming. We have so far agreed that this is a true interpretation, though with the qualification that more emphasis should be placed on the fact that, as Jesus conceives it, God is already at work in him in a way which is organically related to the future event. The powers of the Kingdom are proleptically operative in Jesus, although its coming remains a decisive act of the future. We agree then that on the whole Bultmann's interpretation is true so far as it goes. *So far as it goes*, for it goes no further than the public part of the first half of the ministry of Jesus. There are of course very good grounds for Bultmann's refusal to go further. For to a radical form-critic it is impossible to go further. The Markan narrative is simply a fortuitous agglomeration of *pericopae* prefaced to a Passion narrative. Any traces of development which we may discern in the Markan narrative are due, not to a genuine historical tradition, but to the evangelist himself. He has produced this apparent development either by the *arrangement* of the *pericopae* which he had received from tradition—as for instance when he places Peter's Confession at Caesarea Philippi in the centre of the earthly ministry instead of after the Resurrection—or by his own *editorial constructions*, as for instance in the prophecies of the Passion. In effect, however, Bultmann's procedure is to select out of Mark's supposedly fortuitous agglomeration certain elements, viz., the proclamation of Jesus with its accompanying signs and teaching, and to pronounce these and these alone to be historical. But these elements are significantly confined to the period before Caesarea Philippi or to what is consistent with it. Bultmann then uses Mark 1.1-8.26 as a criterion to judge Mark 8.27-end. In this way he can eliminate all the teaching Jesus is recorded to have given about his impending death. Although Bultmann apparently accepts the historicity of the Crucifixion,[1] he jumps in effect from the Galilean preaching of Jesus to the Jerusalem preaching of the earliest Church. This is a very cavalier procedure, and we may ask whether it is possible to dismiss the Markan order bag and baggage like this, and whether Bultmann really offers an intelligible reconstruction of the events which led to the emergence of the primitive *ecclesia* and its *kerygma*.

I. THE VALUE OF THE MARKAN ORDER

The form critics have done valuable work in classifying certain types of *pericopae*, such as the pronouncement stories, the miracles, and the different forms of teaching. But like all pioneers who discover a new method, they think their discovery is the clue to all truth and work it to death, applying it even where it is no longer applicable. This is what has happened in their treatment of the Baptism and Temptation and of the Confession at Caesarea Philippi and the Transfiguration. To classify the latter two as misplaced Resurrection appearances, and the former two as 'legends' is really a confession of failure. These episodes elude ordinary form-critical treatment. We may indeed regard it as an assured result of form criticism that such classes of material as pronouncement stories, miracle stories, parables and aphorisms were handed down as isolated units and took their shape in the various activities of the Church, catechetical, liturgical, etc. For they are essentially illustrative in character: they belong to quite a general class, and one example could easily be substituted for another. But with these four events we are considering the case is quite different. They are not general examples of our Lord's teaching

[1] *Theology*, p. 20.

or healing, which might equally be replaced by other examples. Rather, they have unique irreplaceability which gives them a certain biographical significance in the life of Jesus. Of course the word 'biographical' is to a form critic like a red rag to a bull! Yet it must surely be admitted that the Passion narrative, while told as *kerygma*, and not as biography, does possess a certain biographical character. It is related with some sense of the sequence of events, and it is precisely because it is a part of the biography of Jesus that the Passion possesses kerygmatic value at all. Now the *kerygma* not only contained a Passion narrative, but was prefaced with an outline of the ministry of Jesus (Acts 2.22-24, 10.36-43) consisting not only of a generalized summary of his activity ('a man approved of God unto you by mighty works and wonders and signs'—'went about doing good, and healing all that were oppressed of the devil'), but also a distinct reference to the anointing of Jesus at his Baptism ('after the baptism which John preached; even Jesus of Nazareth, how that God anointed him with the Holy Ghost and with power'). Clearly then, the Baptism of Jesus belongs to the earliest stratum of the New Testament tradition, to the '*kerygma* of the earliest Church'. Bultmann of course is fully aware that the Baptism of Jesus by John was in itself an historical fact[1] but contends that Mark (or his Hellenistic predecessors who shaped the oral tradition) has refashioned the story into a 'legend' by working in the Voice from Heaven and the descent of the Spirit in order to express the Hellenistic notion that Jesus was a 'divine man' during his earthly life. As a matter of fact however, the theology which the Voice from Heaven and the descent of the Spirit serve to express is neither the invention of Mark nor 'Hellenistic'. It already appears in the allusion to the Baptism just cited from Acts 10.38 (a kerygmatic passage), and represents a genuinely Hebraic, biblical theology—the theology of the Suffering Servant—as the following tables will make clear:

[1] *Theology*, p 26. That Jesus should have submitted to a baptism εἰς ἄφεσιν ἁμαρτιῶν occasioned so many difficulties—cf. Matt. 3.14-15 and the apocryphal versions of the story—that it can hardly have been a Christian invention.

| Behold my servant ... my *chosen* in whom my soul *delighteth*: I *have put my spirit upon him* (Isa. 42.1) | The spirit of the Lord God is upon me; because *the Lord hath anointed me* (Isa. 61.1) Oh that thou wouldest *rend the heavens* (Isa. 64.1) | καὶ εὐθέως ἀναβαίνων ἐκ τοῦ ὕδατος εἶδε σχιζομένους τοὺς οὐρανούς, καὶ τὸ πνεῦμα ὡς περιστερὰν καταβαῖνον ἐπ᾽ αὐτόν· καὶ φωνὴ ἐγένετο ἐκ τῶν οὐρανῶν, Σὺ εἶ ὁ υἱός μου ὁ ἀγαπητός, ἐν σοὶ εὐδόκησα (Mark 1.10-11) | ὡς ἔχρισεν αὐτὸν πνεύματι ἁγίῳ καὶ δυνάμει (Acts 10.38) |

It is reasonable therefore to infer that Mark's account of the Baptism of Jesus did not originate as an isolated Hellenistic legend, but was part of the preface to the Passion in the earliest *kerygma*, and interpreted the earthly life of Jesus as a life of Sonship defined, not in terms of the Hellenistic 'divine man', but in terms of the Spirit-endowed Servant of Isaiah. Bultmann would seem to be mistaken both about the theology of the Markan account of the Baptism, and about the history of its transmission. And if he is wrong about the Baptism, may he not be wrong about the Transfiguration as well? For there are close affinities between the Transfiguration and the Baptism. In both there is the same feature of the Voice from Heaven, and the utterance of the Voice is expressed in closely similar terms, suggesting the same Isaianic theology. Thus the question arises whether the story of the Transfiguration did not originate in close association with the story of the Baptism, expressing the same theology, and linked, like the Baptism narrative, to the *kerygma*. No doubt the imagery of the Transfiguration narrative has been objectivized (e.g. μετεμορφώθη and the appearances of Moses and Elijah), but its kernel consists of the Voice from Heaven, which, like the Voice at the Baptism, is a reference to Isa. 42.1.[1] If the Transfiguration declares Jesus to be the Isaianic servant, it is not a Resurrection appearance put by Mark in the wrong place, for the description of Jesus in terms of the Servant belongs not to the post-Resurrection period, but to his earthly life.[2] Understood in

---

[1] Jeremias, T.W.N.T., V, p. 699, suggests that Luke's substitution of ἀγαπητός by ἐκλελεγμένος (cf. II Pet. 1.17) is due to a variant translation of בחירי in Isa. 42.1.   [2] See below, pp. 86 ff; 107.

this way, the Transfiguration presents us, like the Baptism, with a theology characteristic of the earliest *kerygma*, and therefore I submit that, like the Baptism, it too belongs to the kerygmatic preface to the Passion briefly sketched, though not fully given, in Acts 2 and 10. But there is an important difference between the two Voices: at the Baptism, according to Mark, the communication of Isa. 42 is addressed to Jesus (σὺ εἶ), while at the Transfiguration it is addressed to the disciples (οὗτός ἐστιν). It would seem therefore that Mark's idea that there was a turning point in the ministry, at which the disciples were initiated into the future destiny of Jesus, is not his own invention, but was something contained in the earliest tradition about Jesus, namely that of the *kerygma* of the Aramaic-speaking Church at Jerusalem, which interpreted the earthly life of Jesus in terms of the Isaianic servant (Acts 3.13, 26, 4. 27, 30). Now the Confession of Peter at Caesarea Philippi is also connected with the Transfiguration by the unusual temporal link in Mark 9.2, μετὰ ἡμέρας ἕξ. Where Mark constructs editorial links of his own he is normally content with a simple καί or a vague chronological link like δι᾽ ἡμερῶν (2.1) or ἐν ἐκείναις ταῖς ἡμέραις (8.1). This seems to show that the link here was not constructed by Mark (cf. the links within the Passion narrative), but that the Confession and the Transfiguration were already connected together in his source. That Caesarea Philippi is the turning point at which Jesus 'began' (Mark 8.31) to initiate his disciples into the fact and purpose of his impending death does not appear to be a Markan invention, and therefore it cannot be dismissed so lightly as Bultmann does.[1]

The other and more general objection to Bultmann's reconstruction of the history of Jesus is that he offers no bridge between the public proclamation of the imminent advent of the Kingdom of God in Galilee, and the death of Jesus at Jerusalem. Why should an eschatological prophet go up to Jerusalem deliberately to die? If all the other activity of Jesus was controlled by his proclamation of the coming Kingdom,

[1] For the idea of a sketch of the ministry as a kerygmatic preface to the Passion story, cf. also Wilfred L. Knox, *The Sources of the Synoptic Gospels*, Vol. I, 1953, pp. 2 ff, a book which appeared too late to be used here.

what was the relation between that proclamation and his death? The earliest *kerygma* itself offered an answer in its assertion that Jesus was 'delivered up *by the determinate counsel and foreknowledge of God*' (Acts 2.23). Had Jesus himself no answer to that question? If he was careful to relate his healings and exorcisms to his proclamation, it is surely incredible that he did not relate his death to it also. Yet Bultmann never so much as raises the question, except to dismiss all the prophecies of the Passion as editorial constructions.[1] But without them it is impossible to make sense of the history of Jesus. To these therefore we now turn.

2. THE PROPHECIES OF THE PASSION

There are five prophecies of the Passion in the Markan narrative, all of which are placed after the Confession of Peter at Caesarea Philippi, an event which, as we have argued represented a turning point in the ministry of Jesus, not only in the mind of Mark, but also in the pre-Markan tradition and, with a high degree of probability, in the preface to the Passion in the earliest *kerygma*. These five sayings are as follows:

8.31. The Son of man *must suffer many things, and be rejected* by the elders, and the chief priests, and the scribes, and *be killed*, and after three days rise again.

9.12. How is it written of the Son of man, *that he should suffer many things and be set at nought*?

9.31. The Son of man *is delivered up into the hands of men, and they shall kill him*; and *when he is killed*, after three days he shall rise again.

10.33-34. The Son of man *shall be delivered* unto the chief priests and the scribes; and they shall condemn him to death, and shall deliver him unto the Gentiles; and they shall mock him, and shall spit upon him, and shall scourge him, and *shall kill him*; and after three days he shall rise again.

10.45. The Son of man *came not to be ministered unto, but to minister*, and *to give his life a ransom for many*.

Cf. also Luke 17.25 (peculiar to Luke).

[1] *Theology*, pp. 29 f. On p. 20 he casually suggests that Jesus was crucified as a 'messianic prophet'.

It has often been pointed out[1] that not everything in these sayings need necessarily be rejected as *vaticinia ex eventu*, and of Mark 9.12 in particular Dr. Manson has written[2] that it 'has the rugged and irreducible form of an original oracle'. Following up this hint, we have italicized those portions of the sayings which do not refer to concrete details from the Passion narrative, and which are therefore quite clearly not the result of reflexion on subsequent events.[3] Now it is interesting and significant that these italicized sayings when placed together form a clear description of the Suffering Servant of Isaiah 53:

> [The Son of man] must suffer many things, and be rejected and set at nought, and delivered up into the hands of men and they shall kill him. [For he came] not to be ministered unto, but to minister (=be the servant of Yahweh), and to give his life a ransom for many.

Three of these phrases are generalized summaries of the fate of the Suffering Servant, viz., 'to minister' (which is equivalent to 'fulfilling the mission of the Servant'), and 'suffer many things' and 'be killed'. The other phrases, with one exception, appear to be direct reproductions of the language of the *Hebrew* text of Isa. 53.[4] (i) 'Be set at nought', ἐξουδενωθῇ represents the Hebrew *nibhzeh* at Isa. 53.3 (R.V. 'be despised', LXX ἄτιμον). (ii) 'Be rejected' represents the Hebrew *ḥᵃdhal*

[1] Dodd, *Parables*, p. 57, p. 96; W. Manson, *Messiah*, p. 129
[2] *Loc. cit.*
[3] After considerable hesitation, I have omitted the allusions to the Resurrection from those portions of the predictions which are quite clearly not the result of reflection on subsequent events. It might be argued that only the phrase 'after three days' is a *post eventum* addition, especially since the possibility of resurrection after suffering is suggested by Isa. 53.11-12*a*. Further consideration however suggests that a reference to the Resurrection is not really necessary to the prophecies, since the term 'Son of man' itself is a triumphant, vindicated figure. 'The Son of man must suffer' means that the triumphant, vindicated figure of Dan. 7.13 f must first of all undergo suffering, before he attains to the glory his name implies. It is, in my judgement, improbable that Jesus distinguished between resurrection and exaltation. Resurrection would no doubt appear to him as a necessary preliminary to exaltation after death, but it was the exaltation which was most clearly foretold in scripture, and which was uppermost in his mind. Cf. his reply to the Chief Priest, in which only the vindication, not the Resurrection is mentioned (Mark 14.62). On the other hand, the prophecy of the 'killing' of the Son of Man has been retained as a colourless word. A *post eventum* insertion would surely have mentioned 'crucifixion'.
[4] See Jeremias, T.W.N.T., V, p. 709.

in the same verse (R.V. 'rejected', LXX gives ἐκλεῖπον, which is more literal. Cf. R.V. margin 'forsaken'). But Mark's ἀποδοκιμασθῆναι and R.V. text are both legitimate paraphrases. (iii) 'Give his life a ransom' (δοῦναι τὴν ψυχὴν αὐτοῦ λύτρον) represents the Hebrew *'im tāsîm 'āshām naphshô.* Isa. 53.10 (R.V. 'make his soul an offering for sin'. LXX ἐὰν δῶτε περὶ ἁμαρτίας). λύτρον is a perfectly adequate rendering of *'āshām,* the meaning of which in this passage is given by Brown, Driver and Briggs s.v. as: 'the Messianic servant offers himself as an *'āshām in compensation for the sins of the people, interposing for them as their substitute.*' The authenticity of Mark 10.45 has been widely questioned (most thoroughly by Rashdall[1]) on two grounds: first, on the ground that Luke 22.24-27 represents the original form of the saying about service, and that the λύτρον clause is therefore later in origin; secondly, on the ground that the λύτρον theology is Pauline. But against these arguments it is to be observed, first, that a close comparison of the language of Luke 22.26 with that of Mark 10.45 suggests that the Lukan form is later and secondary. For the two words νεώτερος and ἡγούμενος (Luke 22.26) reflect the concern of the Hellenistic Churches with the differentiation of the members in the local congregation.[2] It would seem that Luke found this saying in his Sayings Source (an expanded form of Q, if we allow this much of truth in the Proto-Luke theory), where the original saying has been modified into a rule for church order, and the λύτρον clause consequently dropped as irrelevant. Secondly, so far from being Pauline, the word λύτρον is distinctly non-Pauline. For Paul never makes use of any of the Servant language, except where he is quoting tradition which he has received from pre-Pauline Christianity. The word λύτρον is entirely absent from Paul, and ἀπολύτρωσις, which does appear, has its background not in the Servant language, but in the Exodus.[3] (iv) 'For many' (ἀντὶ πολλῶν) is perhaps an echo of *lārābbim* (ἀντί=*l*ᵉ) in the Hebrew text of Isa. 53.11 rather than

[1] *The Idea of the Atonement,* 1919, pp. 29 ff, 49 ff.
[2] For ἡγούμενος, cf. Heb. 13.7, 17, 24, and for νεώτερος I Tim. 5.1, 2, 11, 14; I Pet. 5.5.
[3] See further Taylor on Mark 10.45.

of the πολλοῖς or πολλῶν of the LXX in verses 11 and 12 respectively. (v) The expression 'hands of *men*' (Mark 9.31) echoes the *'ishīm* of Isa. 53.3 as those at whose hands the Servant suffers. There remains the one exception to this derivation from the Hebrew Bible mentioned above, viz., the phrase 'be delivered up' (παραδοθῆναι). The verb παραδίδωμι occurs in the LXX at 53.6 and twice in verse 12, but in each case it represents a rather remote paraphrase of the Hebrew original.[1] Either then the use of παραδίδωμι in the prophecies is derived from the LXX, and not from the Hebrew, in which case, like the *post eventum* prophecies, it belongs to the Hellenistic stratum of the tradition, or, if it is pre-Hellenistic, its use is not derived from Isa. 53, but represents a completely non-theological use of the word. The latter seems more probable for two reasons. First, the verb παραδίδωμι appears in connexion with the Passion even in the pre-Hellenistic *kerygma* (Acts 3.13). Secondly, its use is not confined to the Passion of Jesus; it is used, e.g. of John the Baptist (Mark 1.14) and of the persecution of the disciples (Mark 13.9, 11, 12).[2] On the whole, therefore, we may conclude that the use of the verb παραδίδωμι belongs to the earliest stratum of tradition, and, in view of the absence of an equivalent from the Hebrew of Isa. 53, is not derived from that source, but from common secular usage.

The prophecies of the Passion thus contain two strata, a pre-Hellenistic stratum in which Jesus is represented as fore-telling his sufferings partly in general terms and partly in language derived from the Hebrew text of Isa. 53, and a later stratum (whether editorial or pre-Markan, we cannot say for

---

[1] In verse 6 Heb. הִפְגִּיעַ בּוֹ אֵת עֲוֹן כֻּלָּנוּ lit. 'caused to light on him the iniquity of us all' is rendered by the LXX as: παρέδωκεν αὐτὸν ταῖς ἁμαρτίαις αὐτῶν. In verse 12 the first occurrence is: παρεδόθη εἰς θάνατον ἡ ψυχὴ αὐτοῦ, a loose paraphrase of הֶעֱרָה לַמָּוֶת נַפְשׁוֹ, 'he *poured out* his soul unto death'. And the last clause of this verse, διὰ τὰς ἁμαρτίας αὐτῶν παρεδόθη is a loose rendering of לַפֹּשְׁעִים יַפְגִּיעַ 'he makes entreaty for sinners'.

[2] Cf. F. Büchsel, T.W.N.T., II, p. 172: 'The frequent occurrence of the verb in the Passion narrative is not surprising, since it is the normal word used in connexion with legal trials and martyrdoms. . . . Heb. equivalent is מָסַר.' Note the absence of מָסַר from Isa. 53: Büchsel makes no reference to Isa. 53 in his discussion of παραδίδωμι.

certain) in which the prophecies have been expanded in the light of subsequent events. The more primitive stratum in these predictions cannot be dismissed as editorial constructions or as products of Hellenistic Christianity.[1] They originate in a milieu in which the Hebrew Old Testament, rather than the LXX was in use. They therefore belong at least to the same stratum as the *kerygma* of the Aramaic-speaking Church at Jerusalem. Can we press them back further? Can we say with certainty that they represent the teaching of Jesus himself? This is a question which in the nature of the case it is not possible to answer conclusively, for in a very real sense it is not possible to get back behind the apostolic witness. But we can at least hope to answer it with a high degree of probability, and with that hope we press our investigations further. Are there other indications that Jesus interpreted his death in the light of Isa. 53, or are there any indications of another, alternative interpretation which has a higher claim to historicity?

At this point it will be an advantage to consider two sayings which occur in the material peculiar to Luke. The first of these is:

> I came to cast fire upon the earth; and what will I, if it is already kindled? But I have a baptism to be baptized with; and how am I straitened till it be accomplished! Luke 12.49-50.

The authenticity of this saying has been assailed on three grounds. First, it is held to be a *vaticinium ex eventu*.[2] Against this it is sufficient to quote the words of Dr. B. S. Easton[3]: 'The Hebraic construction is proof that this saying was not written by Luke [against Loisy] if proof were needed; J. W[eiss] notes that the extreme indirectness of the reference to the Passion is almost positive evidence of originality.'[4] Secondly, it has been held that the use of 'baptism' as a metaphor for

---

[1] Kümmel, *Verheissung*, pp. 63 f, adds Luke 17.25 to the more original predictions of the Passion. But it is probably editorial.
[2] Bultmann, *Tradition*, p. 165; Loisy, *Les Evangiles Synoptiques* 1, pp. 890 ff.
[3] *St. Luke, ad loc.*
[4] Cf. also Flemington, *Baptism*, p. 31; Taylor, *Sacrifice*, p. 166.

martyrdom reflects the terminology of the later Church.[1] This is highly improbable, for the use of baptism as a metaphor for martyrdom is not attested earlier than Irenaeus.[2] And in any case the death of Jesus was not regarded by the early Christians as a martyrdom, but placed in a unique category of its own. Thirdly, it has been held that the use of baptism as a metaphor for death in this Lukan passage reflects the Hellenistic or Pauline doctrine of baptism as a dying with Christ (Rom. 6.1-11; Col. 2.12), which in turn is held to be derived from a gnostic redemption myth and the concomitant belief in sacramental identification with the fate of the cult deity.[3] Now although the affinity between the Pauline doctrine of baptism as an identification with the death of Christ with similar rites in the mystery religions is undeniable,[4] yet there are indications that the connexion of baptism with the death of Christ is both pre-Pauline and pre-Hellenistic. (i) Paul's introduction of the theme at Rom. 6.3 with the words ἢ ἀγνοεῖτε suggests that he is appealing to a common tradition, quite probably to an element in the original preaching which he could assume the missionaries had delivered when they first preached to the Roman Church. In view of Paul's emphatic claim that his own *kerygma* was substantially identical with that of the Jerusalem apostles (1 Cor. 15.11), it would seem that the connexion of baptism with the death of Christ was common to all forms of the *kerygma*, Palestinian, Hellenistic and Pauline alike. (ii) The earliest *kerygma* of the Jerusalem apostles concluded with the appeal: 'Repent, and be baptized every one of you in the name of Jesus Christ.' Baptism 'in the name of Jesus Christ' would surely involve an identification of the convert with the whole redemptive work of Jesus proclaimed in the *kerygma*. It is 'a concrete embodiment of the apostolic preaching'.[5] Hence the Pauline doctrine that baptism means a dying with Christ would seem to have its roots, not in any gnostic myth or mystery rite, but in the preaching and practice of the earliest Church, which already connected

[1] Cf. A. Oepke, T.W.N.T., I, p. 536.   [2] Oepke, *ibid.*
[3] Bultmann, *Tradition, ibid.*; cf. *Theology*, pp. 140 ff.
[4] Cullmann, *Baptism*, p. 14, footnote 2.
[5] Flemington, *Baptism*, p. 50.

baptism with the death of Jesus. Thus there is no reason to see in Luke 12.49-50 the product of a gnosticizing Hellenistic Christianity. Moreover, if Jesus had already spoken of his death as a baptism, as Luke 12.49 f asserts—and cf. also Mark 10.38 f: the linking of baptism and death has a double attestation—then the primitive practice of baptism in the name of Jesus and the doctrine of Rom. 6 have an intelligible basis. Indeed, the death of Jesus as a baptism is a category running through the whole New Testament, and we may say with a tolerable degree of certainty that it has its origins in the teaching of our Lord himself.

Now the clue to the meaning of the sayings in Luke 12.49 f, with their reference to 'fire' and to 'baptism', surely lies in the Baptism of Jesus himself by John. The pronouncement story recorded in Mark 11.27-33 suggests that Jesus believed that the source of that authority ($\dot{\epsilon}\xi o v\sigma\dot{\iota}a$) by which he did 'these things', i.e. not merely the immediately preceding activity, but his ministry as a whole,[1] lay in his Baptism by John. The Baptism of Jesus by John, however, as we have seen, gave him the authority specifically to fulfil the mission of the Servant of Isaiah.[2] This mission began with the proclamation of the coming Reign of God, and with the performance of the signs which were subordinated to that proclamation. But the Servant's mission was not exhausted by that activity. There still remained the suffering of Isa. 50 and 53, which was therefore already implicit in the Voice at the Baptism. In speaking of his death as a 'baptism' Jesus therefore means the fulfilment of his Baptism by John when he entered upon the vocation of the Servant. There is still the problem of the meaning of the 'fire' in the earlier part of the saying. Most commentators seem to be at a loss how to take it. Many[3] connect it with the sayings about conflict which follow in Luke 12.51 ff, taking it to mean 'the fire of discord'. But verses 51-53 belong to a different tradition (Q) from verses 49-50 (special Luke), and their combination is secondary. Moreover, as Dr. V. Taylor points out,[4] this interpretation does not agree with the longing

---

[1] See Manson, *Messiah*, p. 40; Schniewind, *Mark, ad loc.*
[2] See above p. 53f.   [3] e.g. Easton, *ad loc.*   [4] *Sacrifice*, p. 165.

expressed in verse 49*b*. On the other hand Dr. Taylor's own suggestions, 'the fire of righteousness', or alternatively, 'the fire of holiness', are equally unconvincing. Surely the clue to the meaning lies in the reference to 'baptism' in verse 50, and in the warning of John: 'He shall baptize you with fire.'[1] The fire that Jesus has come to cast is therefore the fire of the eschatological judgement, the negative aspect of the coming of the Kingdom (cf. Mark 9.49). And this, as the next verse shows, will be accomplished in the death which he will die in fulfilment of the mission of the Servant inaugurated at his Baptism. The ministry of Jesus is therefore not exhausted in the proclamation of the coming Reign of God. It is his destiny also to accomplish the event by which that Reign should be inaugurated. The interpretation of the death of Jesus is the same here as that implied by the predictions of the Passion examined above, viz., an interpretation in terms of Isa. 53, but with the difference that here the death thus interpreted is brought directly into relation with the proclamation of the coming Reign of God.

The second saying about the Passion peculiar to Luke is the answer to Herod:

> Go and say to that fox, Behold, I cast out devils and perform cures to-day and to-morrow, and the third day I am perfected. Howbeit I must go on my way to-day and to-morrow and the day following: for it cannot be that a prophet perish out of Jerusalem (Luke 13.32 f).

Since Wellhausen's argument that 'on the third day I am perfected' in verse 32, and 'to-day and to-morrow' in verse 33 are interpolations is widely accepted as producing a smoother text,[2] it would be precarious to attach much importance to τελειοῦμαι in verse 32 in any attempt to reconstruct Jesus' own interpretation of his death. We will therefore confine ourselves to what remains: 'Behold, I cast out devils and perform cures

---

[1] This is probably the original form of the saying at Mark 1.8; Matt. 3.11 = Luke 3.16. The substitution of πνεῦμα in Mark and the addition of it in Matthew and Luke (?Q) is a reflection of later Christian experience. See Barrett, *Spirit*, pp. 125 f.

[2] See e.g. Easton and Creed, *ad loc.*, though contrast Taylor, *Sacrifice*, pp. 170 f.

to-day and to-morrow. Howbeit I must go on my way the day following: for it cannot be that a prophet perish out of Jerusalem.' The first point to be noticed in this saying is that Jesus expressly and publicly declares that his mission is not exhausted in the exorcisms and healings of the earlier part of his ministry. There is a 'must', a δεῖ, which extends further than healing and exorcism, the signs which buttress the proclamation of the imminent advent of God's Reign, a 'must' which extends to his dying at Jerusalem. This indubitably authentic saying, free as it is from the slightest suspicion of *Gemeindetheologie*, is the clearest proof we could desire of the inadequacy of Bultmann's reconstruction of the history of Jesus. By stating that it is as a 'prophet' that he is to perish at Jerusalem, Jesus brings his death into organic relation with his prophetic proclamation, 'the Reign of God has drawn nigh'. The question arises here, however, whether we have not the original, authentic interpretation which Jesus placed upon his death (viz., that he was to die simply as a *prophet*, like John the Baptist). Is the Servant interpretation of his death after all a product of the Church, albeit the earliest Aramaic-speaking Church at Jerusalem? Certainly, martyrdom was widely associated with the prophetic vocation.[1] There are, however, three features in this saying which suggest that Jesus, even here, meant to imply that his death had a deeper significance than the martyrdom of a mere prophet. First, it must be remembered that this saying is a public one, addressed to 'certain Pharisees' (Luke 13.31). We may reasonably suspect that Jesus, who reserved the deeper mysteries of his vocation to his more intimate disciples, deliberately restricted himself in public to a limited interpretation of his mission, which nevertheless was true as far as it went. Secondly, precisely because he says he must die as a prophet, Jesus is bringing his death into organic relation with his prophetic proclamation and its accompanying healings and exorcisms. But, as we have already seen, his prophetic proclamation and his healings and exorcisms were part of the *dawning* of the Reign of God

[1] See e.g. the parable of the Vineyard, Mark 12.4 f para.; also Matt. 22.6, 23.30 f para., 37 para. and cf. Jeremias T.W.N.T., V, p. 711.

and part of his mission as the Servant in fulfilment of Isa.
61.1.[1] Therefore this reference to his dying as a prophet, so
far from excluding an organic connexion with the dawning of
the Reign of God, and so far from excluding the Servant interpretation, actually suggests these things to those who were
'in the know', who had eyes to see and ears to hear. Thirdly,
why this insistence that as a prophet he must perish at Jerusalem? True, Jerusalem had repeatedly killed the prophets in
the course of her history (verse 34). But to perish at Jerusalem
was not an invariable feature of the prophetic vocation, for
John the Baptist, although acknowledged by Jesus to be at
least a prophet, if not more (Matt. 11.9) had perished outside
of Jerusalem. It may be that the meaning behind this insistence
that he must perish at Jerusalem is that Jerusalem is the place
of revelation, the centre from which the redemptive activity
of God is to go forth to the world,[2] and that therefore the
death of Jesus is to be the culmination of the sacred history of
God's dealings with his people.[3] At all events, this Lukan
saying cannot be exploited to prove that Jesus interpreted his
death as a prophetic martyrdom, and nothing more. It is
perfectly compatible with the view that he went up to Jerusalem with the deliberate intention of fulfilling the role of the
Suffering Servant of Isa. 53 as the decisive event by which the
coming of the Kingdom, whose imminent advent he had
proclaimed in Galilee, should be accomplished.

3. THE LAST SUPPER

It is curious that Bultmann defers all consideration of the
Last Supper until he comes to pre-Pauline Hellenistic Christianity.[4] Presumably, though he does not say so, he regards
the tradition of the Last Supper as an aetiological cult myth.
As a matter of fact, however, there is hardly anything in the
New Testament which is better and more early attested than
the narrative of the Last Supper. To begin with, we have

[1] Cf. the Reply to John, Matt. 11.2 ff, and see above, pp. 20 ff, 35 ff.
[2] Cf. A. G. Hebert, *The Throne of David*, 1941, pp. 214 ff.
[3] Cf. Mark 12.6 para.
[4] *Theology*, pp. 144 ff.

earlier written evidence of this narrative than of any other episode in the life of Jesus, for Paul's account in I Cor. 11.23-25 was written not later than 55. But this, as Paul says, was part of the *paradosis* which he had received from the Church before him (verse 23: ἐγὼ γὰρ παρέλαβον ἀπὸ τοῦ κυρίου[1]). Paul must therefore have received this account previous to A.D. 50, the date when he handed it over to the Corinthians at their conversion. How much earlier? Jeremias dismisses the possibility that Paul received it at the time of his conversion[2] and suggests that I Cor. 11.23-25 represents the tradition current at Antioch in A.D. 40, when Paul made his quarters there (Acts 11.26). He rejects the possibility of an earlier origin for two reasons. First, the language of I Cor. 11.23-25 suggests a Hellenistic revision in which the earlier Semitisms have been ironed out. Second, it shows affinities with the longer Lukan text, which in Professor Jeremias' view is original and independent of I Cor. 11.23-25. Both of these reasons are open to question. First, may not the revision of the Greek have been done by Paul himself? The phraseology of the cup-word is characteristically Pauline: 'This cup is the *new covenant* in my blood.' The theology of the two covenants is fundamental to Paul's interpretation of salvation history[3] and the Church's

---

[1] H. Lietzmann, *Messe und Herrenmahl*, 1926, p. 255, favoured direct revelation. Cf. also his *An die Korinther ad loc.*: 'If he were quoting human authorities, he would say παρά'. This view is now generally abandoned, as is indicated by Kümmel's dissent from Lietzmann's view in his revised (1949) edition of Lietzmann's commentary cited above, p. 185: 'By παρέλαβον ἀπὸ τοῦ κυρίου Paul doubtless means not the understanding of the account of the Last Supper disclosed to him in the Damascus revelation, but the tradition about the Last Supper which goes back ultimately to the Lord. The reason why he uses ἀπό here instead of παρά, is probably a desire to emphasize that the κύριος is to be regarded not as guarantor behind the chain of tradition, but as its ultimate source.' Jeremias (*Abendmahlsworte*, pp. 95 f) puts forward the following additional arguments in favour of this interpretation: (i) The terms παραλαμβάνειν and παραδιδόναι represent קבל מן and מסר ל, the regular Rabbinic terms for the handing on of a tradition from one Rabbi to another. (ii) Where Paul uses the identical introduction at I Cor. 15.3, the ensuing kerygmatic formula is strikingly un-Pauline in its language, and betrays signs of Aramaic origin. See Higgins, *Lord's Supper*, p. 26, for an imposing array of modern scholars who accept this exegesis of I Cor. 11.23. Even Bultmann considers I Cor. 11.23 ff to represent a *pre-Pauline*, albeit Hellenistic Christian tradition (*Theology*, pp. 44 ff).

[2] *Abendmahlsworte*, p. 97.

[3] See Gal. 4.24 ff; II Cor. 3.6 ff; and cf. Behm, T.W.N.T., II, p. 132 f.

ministry is for him essentially the διακονία τῆς καινῆς διαθήκης. We may therefore infer that Paul himself revised the cup-word.[1] Secondly, as we shall try to prove later,[2] the longer Lukan text is secondary. The way is thus clear for the possibility that Paul received the tradition of the Lord's Supper immediately after his conversion when he joined the Church at Damascus. The general reluctance to accept this possibility is that it is thought to be inconsistent with what Paul reports of his movements after his conversion in Gal. 1.15-17. But Paul is not giving here a complete biography of his early life as a Christian. What he is asserting is that his apostolic mission began and proceeded without any authorization from those who were apostles before him. When Paul says that after his conversion 'immediately I conferred not with flesh and blood' he does not mean that he avoided all human contact (e.g. that he withdrew at once to a hermit's existence in Arabia). He means that he did not seek *authorization* from 'flesh and blood' (cf. Gal. 1.1 οὐκ ἀπ' ἀνθρώπων οὐδὲ δι' ἀνθρώπου). The narrative in Acts 9.8-22 of Paul's visit to Damascus, of his baptism by Ananias and his preaching in Damascus is not inconsistent with the claim of Gal. 1.15-17. Paul's baptism by Ananias was not the kind of contact with flesh and blood that he was speaking of in Gal. 1.16 (for he was there speaking of the authorization of his apostolic mission, which according to Acts 9.15 also came direct from the Lord, and had nothing to do with his baptism by Ananias). And his departure to Arabia (Gal. 1.17) is not contradicted by the statement of Acts that he began preaching in Damascus. It was Paul's practice to use a city as the base for his missionary work in a wide district around. So later he uses Tarsus, Antioch and Ephesus in turn. The accounts of Galatians and Acts are perfectly consistent if we suppose that immediately after his conversion Paul used Damascus in the same way as his centre for missionary work in Arabia Nabatea (hence incidentally incurring the hostility of Aretas, II Cor. 11.32 f) during the years 33-35. Now it could hardly be claimed that the Church of Damascus knew nothing of the Eucharist, that Paul heard of it and of the tradition about

---

[1] Cf. Higgins, *Lord's Supper*, p. 34.   [2] See below, p. 67 f.

the Last Supper only when he made Antioch his headquarters *c.* 40, and that consequently it was only from that date that he began to introduce the Eucharist into his Churches. Such a development is incredible. There would therefore seem no valid reason why Paul should not have 'received' the tradition of the Last Supper already in 33 from the Church of Damascus, even if the exact wording given in I Cor. 11 represents Paul's own recension of the original tradition he received. Now Jeremias has convincingly demonstrated that the Markan version of the Institution is more primitive than Paul's.[1] If this be so, the Markan account of the Institution must represent a tradition substantially identical with that current at Damascus *c.* 33, and therefore belongs to the earliest stratum of the New Testament, contemporaneous with the *kerygma* of the earliest Church. The shorter text of Luke at 22.15-19*a* is not generally regarded nowadays as a serious competitor to the Markan version. Views differ as to its origin. Professor G. D. Kilpatrick[2] argued that the shorter text was original, and that Luke deliberately suppressed the rest of the bread-word and the cup-word to avoid profanation. Jeremias[3] maintains that the longer text is original to Luke, and that the shorter text was produced at the beginning of the second century, and then found its way into part of the Western textual tradition. At the same time Jeremias agrees with Kilpatrick that the motive at work was the desire to avoid profanation of the eucharistic mystery. But if it was desired to suppress the mystery, the job was only half done, for the bread-word is given *in toto* in its Markan form, and only the cup-word is suppressed. Clearly, some other motive must have been at work, affecting the cup but not the bread. If we follow Professor Kil-

---

[1] *Abendmahlsworte*, pp. 88 ff. His reason are highly technical and depend on the presence of some twenty Semitisms in the Markan version which for the most part have been smoothed out in the Pauline version. Dalman (*Jesus-Jeshuah*, p. 145) had already made a similar though less thorough attempt in the same direction. Even Bultmann agrees that the Markan version is more primitive than Paul's, *Theology*, p. 146. Kümmel, *Verheissung*, 113 considers the Pauline cup-word more primitive and the Markan cup-word to be due to assimilation to the bread-word. But the tendency is for the cup- and bread-words to *diverge* through the accumulation of interpretative additions.

[2] J.T.S., XLVII, pp. 49-56.

[3] *Ibid.*, 70 ff.

patrick, and suppose that it was Luke, not a second-century scribe, who was responsible for the suppression, the reason is clear enough. Unlike the other gospels, Luke was avowedly intended, not for use in Church, but for the instruction of catechumens (Luke 1.1 ff) and probably also for apologetic purposes. In other words, it was addressed to a public on the fringe of and outside the Church. This would explain why Luke has suppressed the cup-word. The command to drink the 'blood' of Christ would have been all too easily misunderstood by outsiders, and have given rise to or encouraged just those false charges which were in fact levelled against the early Church by the pagan world.[1] The subsequent lengthening of the shorter text is then more easily accountable than the abbreviation of the longer text, if we suppose that in the second century the Lukan Gospel was adopted, like the other gospels, for Church use, and that the Church which adopted it naturally supplemented the bread-word and added the cup-word *from its own liturgical tradition* (which would account at once for the similarities and for the differences between the longer Lukan version on the one hand, and the Pauline version in I Cor. 11 on the other). In any case therefore, we cannot use the shorter Lukan text, as scholars were prone to do a generation ago, as a proof that the Last Supper originally had no connexion with the Christian Eucharist, or that Luke was following an earlier and better tradition which attributed no redemptive significance to the death of Jesus. For the doctrine of the vicarious sacrifice of Christ is present elsewhere in the Lukan writings.[2] And in no case does the shorter Lukan text represent a competitor to the Markan account. In fact, as the bread-word shows, it actually presupposes the Markan version, and takes it for granted.

This leaves the way clear therefore for an examination of the Markan tradition of the eucharistic words as the earliest tradition we have (A.D. *c.* 33). There are three interpretative sayings which must engage our attention:

[1] Cf. Dalman, *Jesus-Jeshuah*, p. 156.
[2] Jeremias (*Abendmahlsworte*, p. 78, footnote 8) calls attention to Luke's use of Isa. 53 at Luke 22.37; Acts 8.32 ff, 3.13, 26, 4.27, 30 (παῖς), 3.14, 7.52, 22.14 (δίκαιος, from Isa. 53.11).

(i) *The bread-word*: This is my body.

(ii) *The cup-word*: This is my blood of the covenant, which is shed for many.

(iii) *The 'eschatological prospect'*: Verily I say unto you, I will no more drink of the fruit of the vine, until that day when I drink it new in the kingdom of God. Mark 14.22-25.

There is a distinct tendency as time goes on to add interpretative additions to the words over the elements. Thus Matthew adds 'for the remission of sins' to the cup-word, Paul adds 'which is for you' to the bread-word (later MSS. also add 'broken' or 'given'), and the longer Lukan text adds 'which is given for you' to the bread-word, and 'which is shed for you' to the cup-word. Has the same tendency already been at work in the Markan account? If so, then the words 'of the covenant, which is shed for many' must be an added interpretation. If they are subtracted, the parallelism between the bread- and cup-words is perfect.[1] But the interpretative addition must have been made before A.D. *c.* 33, that is, before the Markan and Pauline traditions began to diverge, since the 'covenant' appears in both traditions. Jeremias[2] argues that the phrase 'of the covenant' could only have been added when the tradition had reached Greek-speaking soil. For the wording τὸ αἷμά μου τῆς διαθήκης, harsh enough in Greek, is quite impossible in Aramaic, since in the latter a noun with a prenominal suffix cannot be followed by a genitive. This of course is true enough. Yet there is a perfectly normal way of expressing a phrase of this kind in Aramaic, namely by the use of the prepositional prefix *d^e*, a construction which appears at Dan. 2.34:

rāghlôhî dî phărz^elā' w^eḥăspā' its feet of iron and clay

Dalman sees no difficulty over the Markan form of the cup-word, and uses precisely this idiom when he translates it into Aramaic:

dēn (hāden) hū idmî delikeyāmā[3]

---

[1] Cf. Bultmann, *Theology*, p. 146.   [2] *Abendmahlsworte*, p. 99.

[3] Dalman, *Jesus-Jeshuah*, p. 160. I am informed by Professor H. F. D. Sparks, to whom I am also indebted for the reference to Dan. 2.34, that the Peshitta employs the same idiom at Mark 14.24.

There is a similarly awkward and closely parallel Greek construction in the LXX at Gen. 9.5: τὸ ὑμέτερον αἷμα τῶν ψυχῶν ὑμῶν. This is translation Greek for the Hebrew: *'ĕth-dimᵉkhĕm lᵉnăphshōthêkhĕm* where again we have a noun with prenominal suffix followed by another noun prefixed by *lᵉ* in order to express the genitive relation. So far then from ruling out the possibility of an Aramaic original, the awkward Greek of the Markan form of the covenant saying is best accounted for on that supposition. Consequently, the interpretative addition must have been the work of the earliest Aramaic-speaking Church. Against the further phrase τὸ ἐκχυννόμενον ὑπερ πολλῶν there are no linguistic difficulties against an Aramaic origin.[1] If therefore both parts of the interpretative addition were the work of the earliest Aramaic-speaking Church, were they a product of its own theologizing, or had they any sanction from something Jesus may have said, though not directly attached to the cup-word?

Now the Last Supper was either the actual passover meal of that year[2] or an anticipation of the passover. Jeremias has conclusively demonstrated that every alternative theory which has been proposed (sabbath-kiddush, passover-kiddush, the harmonizing theory of Strack and Billerbeck, and chaburah) is untenable, but his attempt to prove that it was the passover is not conclusive. For, as Dr. V. Taylor, in a judicious examination of the arguments adduced by Jeremias,[3] concludes, surely with every justification: 'We may recognize a certain force when this or that irregularity is defended by an appeal to later Rabbinical decisions, but when this argument is repeated six times over, it wears rather thin' (p. 667). We are left therefore with the possibility of an anticipated passover.[4] Higgins is quite unjustified in dismissing Preiss's solution, without argument, as 'unconvincing',[5] and Jeremias' objection to it on the ground that it was contrary to a law which admitted of no recognized Rabbinic exception[6] is surely not conclusive,

---

[1] Jeremias, *Abendmahlsworte*, p. 99, footnote 5.
[2] So Jeremias, *Abendmahlsworte, passim.*, cf. Higgins, *Lord's Supper*, pp. 13 ff.
[3] *Mark*, pp. 664-7.
[4] So Schniewind, *Mark*, p. 180; Théo Preiss, 'Le dernier repas de Jésus fut-il un repas pascal?' in *La Vie en Christ*, 1951.
[5] *Op. cit.*, p. 16. [6] *Abendmahlsworte*, p. 14 and footnote 1.

since Jesus certainly did not hold himself to be bound by the prescriptions of the law in situations where the interests of the coming Kingdom were paramount.[1] If he could dispense with the Sabbath law on occasion, why not also the passover law? As an anticipated passover, however, it is not merely, except in a purely chronological sense, an anticipation of the passover of that year. It is far more: it is an anticipation of the *fulfilment* of the passover in the Kingdom of God.[2] Now the passover meal proper began with a discourse pronounced by the 'celebrant', usually the father of the household, in response to the request of the youngest member present. 'What mean ye by this service?' (Ex. 12.26). In this discourse, known as the *Haggada*[3], the 'celebrant' gave a symbolic interpretation of the elements used, relating them to the events of the Exodus. Now if the Last Supper was, as we have suggested, an antici-pation of the fulfilment of the passover in the Kingdom of God, it is not difficult to suppose that Jesus opened the meal with a discourse corresponding to the *Haggada*, relating the elements, not of course to the Exodus of the Old Testament, but to its fulfilment in the coming of the Kingdom. There was certainly a tradition that Jesus discoursed at length during the Last Supper,[4] and what would have been more likely than that the bald announcement over the elements during their administration should have been preceded by a discourse in which the otherwise barely intelligible words 'This is my body' and 'This is my blood' were already explained beforehand? In that case the 'words of administration' merely summarized and recalled what had already been said in the discourse. If this possibility is accepted, the interpretative addition to the word over the cup, 'of the covenant which is shed for many', will have been added by the earliest Aramaic-speaking Church, not from its own theologizing, but from the previous explanation of the significance which Jesus had attributed to the elements in his

---

[1] See e.g. Mark 2.23 ff, 3.1 ff; Luke 13.10 ff, 14.1 ff. Jesus' breaches of the law were never due to an unprincipled 'liberalism': they were invariably a concession to the over-riding claims of the Kingdom of God.

[2] So Preiss and Schniewind, *ibid*.

[3] Jeremias, *Abendmahlsworte*, p. 30, p. 48.

[4] Cf. esp. Luke 22.15-16, 24-32; also Mark 14.17-21 and the Farewell Dis-courses of the Fourth Gospel.

preceding discourse at the Last Supper. This suggestion, while not susceptible of conclusive proof, may at least increase our confidence in taking the 'interpretative addition' as fairly representing the mind of Jesus, if not his *ipsissima verba*.[1]

We proceed now to examine the meaning of the Markan sayings at the Supper, in order to amplify what we have already established about the interpretation which Jesus placed upon his impending death.

(i) *This (is) my body: this (is) my blood*

Whatever else Jesus may or may not have meant by these startling and enigmatic words, one thing at least is clear beyond all doubt, and that is that he is relating the elements specifically to the impending event of his *death*. The words which follow (see below) are therefore specifically related to the event of his death and interpretative of it.

(ii) *of the covenant*

It is here that we are to see the central utterance of Jesus which interprets his death.[2] Now according to the Markan form of the cup-saying, the covenant idea is brought into the closest association with the blood ('my blood of the covenant'). This would lead us to seek for the background of the saying in Ex. 24.8 and Zech. 9.11. Paul on the other hand has 'the new covenant in my blood', which recalls Jer. 31.31. If,

---

[1] The so-called 'command to repeat' (I Cor. 11.24b; 25b) may well belong to the same cycle of tradition. Its absence from Mark may be explained from the fact that Mark's purpose in recording the Last Supper is to prefix his Passion narrative with an interpretation of the meaning of the Lord's death and that he is not immediately concerned with the Church's liturgical practice. Paul's purpose on the other hand in I Cor. 11.23-25 is liturgical, and therefore the 'command to repeat' is relevant to his purpose as it is not to Mark's.

[2] Contrast Jeremias, who leaves out the reference to the covenant (107 ff) in his discussion of the interpretation of the Lord's death given by the eucharistic sayings. This is because he regards the words τῆs διαθήκηs as an early theological interpretation added to the original saying (99; see above p. 69). In this he is closely followed by Higgins (*Lord's Supper*, pp. 49 ff), who also ignores the covenant idea in his interpretation of Jesus' death. But there are good reasons for supposing that the covenant idea is original to the mind of Jesus (see below, p. 73 f). Cf. also J. Behm, T.W.N.T., II, pp. 136 f, who, however, regards the Pauline form of the cup-saying as original. F.-J. Leenhardt (*Le sacrement de la sainte cène*, 1948) also gives great prominence to the covenant in his exposition of the Last Supper (pp. 47 f).

however, our argument about the *Haggada* is correct, the saying about the covenant was not originally associated with the actual saying 'this is my blood', but appeared disconnected from it in the explanatory discourse with which the meal was preceded. If this be so, it opens up the possibility that neither Ex. 24.8, Jer. 31.31 nor Zech. 9.11 give us the *immediate* clue to the understanding of the significance of the covenant. Instead, we may find it more directly in the same Servant passages of Deutero-Isaiah, which, as we have already seen, were constitutive and determinative for our Lord's interpretation of his death:

Isa. 42.6: The Lord . . . will . . . give thee (i.e. the Servant of verse 1) for a covenant of the people (cf. Isa. 49.8).

Thus the covenant theology represents no sudden and alien intrusion into the thought of Jesus, no last minute adoption of a totally new conception, but an organic part of the mission of Jesus as it was laid down for him by the Voice at his Baptism. For the Voice of the Father at the Baptism is, as we have seen, a citation of Isa. 42.1[1] and in Rabbinic usage the quotation of the beginning of a text implied the whole of it. It is true that Deutero-Isaiah does not associate the covenant explicitly with the death of the Servant, for the covenant is not mentioned in Isa. 53, but what is more likely than that Jesus himself combined Isa. 42.1 ff and Isa. 52.13 ff into a single all embracing programme for his own mission?

Moreover, the covenant conception is closely allied with the eschatological Kingdom, which as we have seen[2] was the dominant *motif* of the proclamation of Jesus.[3] This relationship between the Kingdom and the covenant is clinched by a logion recorded at Luke 22.29:

I appoint ($\delta\iota\alpha\tau\acute{\iota}\theta\epsilon\mu\alpha\iota$) unto you a kingdom, even as my Father appointed ($\delta\iota\acute{\epsilon}\theta\epsilon\tau o$) unto me.

[1] See above, p. 53 f.   [2] Chapter II.
[3] Cf. J. Behm, T.W.N.T., *loc. cit.*: 'The $\kappa\alpha\iota\nu\grave{\eta}$ $\delta\iota\alpha\theta\acute{\eta}\kappa\eta$ is a conception correlative to $\beta\alpha\sigma\iota\lambda\epsilon\acute{\iota}\alpha$ $\tauo\hat{u}$ $\theta\epsilono\hat{u}$. While the latter designates God as the absolute Lord of the age of redemption, the former is intended to express the sovereign will of God which appoints the goal of his purpose. Both ideas express the *one* goal of fulfilment: "God will reign" and "the new order of God is inaugurated", the order which finally determines the relation between God and man.'

Can we be sure that we have here an authentic saying of Jesus? In the next verse it is followed by a saying which also occurs in a different form and in a different context at Matt. 19.28. Dr. B. S. Easton[1] therefore regards Luke 22.29 as a secondary addition. But it is equally possible that Luke 22.29 forms a detached saying which Luke has combined with verse 30. Otto[2] makes two interesting suggestions at this point. He thinks that verse 29 actually represents the Lukan form of the cup saying which Luke has suppressed (in the shorter version) from the Institution narrative. He also calls attention to the language of Luke 22.29: '*Diatithesthai* means in Hebrew *karath berith* = *diatheken poieisthai*.' I suggest that we have in Luke 22.29 the original form of the covenant saying which was spoken by Jesus at the Last Supper, not over the cup at the distribution, but in the preceding *Haggada*. This was the source from which the earliest Aramaic Church added the covenant saying to the cup-word. In this saying Jesus identifies the covenant which he is about to inaugurate through his death with the Kingdom which had been the subject matter of his proclamation right from the beginning of his ministry.

But at this point the question arises whether the conception of the death of Jesus as the necessary prelude to the coming of the Kingdom is consistent with the teaching which he had given earlier on in his parables. For the parables, and in particular the parable of the Seed Growing Secretly, teach that man cannot hasten the coming of the Kingdom of God.[3] He must be content to wait upon God, who will in his own good time inaugurate the Kingdom by a sheer miracle 'perpendicularly from above'. Has Jesus abandoned this quietism, and decided to force the hand of God by dying a violent death, as Schweitzer thought? The answer is that in speaking of the covenant Jesus interprets his death, not merely as a human act, but as an act in and through which God himself is acting. For to inaugurate a covenant is precisely the prerogative of God alone. It is *God* who concludes the covenant with Noah (Gen. 9.9), with Abraham (Gen. 17.7), with Moses and the people of Israel (Deut. 4.13, etc.). Moreover it is God who

[1] *St. Luke, ad oc.*   [2] *Kingdom*, p. 268.   [3] See above, p. 44 f.

will make the new covenant with his people (Jer. 31.31 and 34). It is God who gives his Servant for a covenant of the people (Isa. 42.6, 49.8). Hence by speaking of his death as the inauguration of a covenant Jesus quite clearly indicates that his death will be no mere human act, but the occasion of a decisive act of God, wrought out on the plane of history in and through his own acceptance of the destiny of the Suffering Servant.

(iii) *which is shed for many*

These words do not add anything to what was inferred from the use of the word 'covenant', but serve to confirm what we have already found. 'Shed' (ἐκχυννόμενον) is a reverential passive, denoting that God is the subject of the action.[1] Jeremias considers that this is directly sacrificial language[2] but the phrase ἐκχεῖν (ἐκχύννειν) αἷμα is very frequently used of bloodshed in general, and may not indicate more than the fact of Jesus' death. If so, then the background of the expression may be sought again in Isa. 53.12b ('he *poured out his soul* unto death'). The added words 'for many' also recall Isa. 53.11, 12 especially *lārābbîm* in verse 11. It is noticeable in each case that the precise formulations of the additional words over the cup are not direct quotations from Isa. 53. The reason for this, we may reasonably conclude, is that Jesus discoursed at length during the Supper about his fulfilment of the figure of the Suffering Servant, and that the earliest Church has produced a succinct summary of his teaching in a concise liturgical formula.

(iv) *Verily I say unto you, I will no more drink of the fruit of the vine, until that day when I drink it new in the kingdom of God.*

As Dr. V. Taylor says[3]: 'The genuineness of this saying needs little discussion. Its ideas are entirely Jewish.' Dalman, however,[4] notes that the word 'new' as a predicate can scarcely be imitated in Aramaic. It may therefore be an interpretative

---

[1] Jeremias, *Abendmahlsworte*, p. 91. He compares Matt. 5.4, 6, 7.
[2] *Abendmahlsworte*, p. 108.   [3] *Sacrifice*, pp. 139 f.   [4] *Jesus-Jeshuah*, p. 182.

addition added to the Greek version of the tradition of the saying. But it is an addition wholly in keeping with the rest of the saying, for the newness referred to is the newness of the Kingdom of God. 'New' is one of the eschatological words of the Bible.[1] Luke has a closely similar saying which he connects with his first cup:

> I will not drink from henceforth of the fruit of the vine, until the kingdom of God shall come (Luke 22.18).

It is scarcely necessary for us to decide which is the original form and context of the logion, though there is much to be said for the view that it was spoken before, rather than after the drinking of wine at the meal. For Jesus explains why he is refraining from partaking of the wine.[2] The phraseology, οὐ μή with the subjunctive, suggests not an oath of renunciation as a reinforcement of his prayer that the Kingdom might come[3] —rather like Gandhi's political fasts!—but rather a solemn resolve to abstain from a particular course of action, as elsewhere in the New Testament.[4] Jesus abstains from the wine, not in order to force the hand of God, but for a different reason. Either he intends his abstention as an expression of his total consecration to the Father's will, in a manner which recalls John 4.34: 'My meat is to do the will of him that sent me, and to accomplish his work.' Or, alternatively, it is an expression of his resolve to drink that other cup (ποτήριον, Mark 14.36), the cup of suffering, to the dregs. It is precisely this consecration to the Father's will, as expressed in his abstention from the cup at Supper, which will make it possible for him to 'drink it new in the kingdom of God' (Mark 14.25b), and which will inaugurate the coming of the Kingdom (Luke 22.18b, cf. verse 16b). In other words, this saying is an addi-

---

[1] See e.g. Mark 1.27, 2.21; John 13.34; II Cor. 3.6, 5.17; Gal. 6.15; Eph. 2.15, 4.24, etc., and cf. Jer. 31.31.
[2] Cf. Dalman, *Jesus-Jeshuah*, p. 155; Jeremias, *Abendmahlsworte*, pp. 118 f; Dodd, *Parables*, p. 60. Contrast Taylor, *Mark, ad loc*. To suppose that Jesus drank of the wine creates a further difficult problem; would he have drunk of the cup which he identified with his blood?
[3] So Jeremias, *Abendmahlsworte*, pp. 118 ff.
[4] Cf. e.g. Mark 14.31: οὐ μή σε ἀπαρνήσωμαι.

tional proof that Jesus regards his death as the decisive event in and through which God will inaugurate the End. That is to say, between Jesus as he sits at Supper and the coming of the Kingdom, there stands the crucial event of the cross.

4. THE CRUCIALITY OF THE CROSS

To interpret Jesus as an eschatological prophet who simply announced the impending advent of the eschatological Reign of God, challenged men to a preparatory decision in face of that impending event, and left it at that, is an entirely inadequate reconstruction of the history of Jesus of Nazareth. The rigid application of the canons of radical form criticism leaves us with an insoluble problem on our hands. Why did Jesus of Nazareth, who in the gospels is always presented as the master of every situation, who did everything with a rigorous concentration of purpose, who subordinated all his activity (proclamation, teaching and signs) to his overriding conviction of the impending advent of the Kingdom of God, expose himself to crucifixion at Jerusalem? This is a question which Bultmann does not, and on his own presuppositions cannot, answer. Once however we are prepared to abandon the extreme conclusions of radical form criticism (recognizing at the same time their *relative* validity within certain limits), and are prepared to place a certain degree of confidence in the order of the Markan narrative, we shall find ourselves able to admit that Mark is historically right in making Caesarea Philippi a turning point in the story of Jesus. From that point onwards Jesus turns from the public proclamation of the advent of the Reign of God and addresses himself to the private initiation of his disciples into the mystery of his impending death. This mystery is that Jesus has been sent not only to announce the coming Reign of God, but to perform the decisive event through which God will inaugurate that Reign. This decisive event Jesus conceives in terms of the fulfilment of the vocation of the Suffering Servant of Isaiah. This interpretation of his death is presented with a remarkable consistency in all the sayings which we have examined, and it is scarcely credible that it is a product even of the earliest Aramaic-speaking Church. For there is no other alternative interpretation discernible anywhere in the sayings of Jesus.[1]

[1] The only possible exception is the saying in Luke 13.33*b*, where Jesus implies that he is going to die merely as a prophet. But there are special reasons for this understatement (see above p. 62 ff). We are not of course contending that Jesus thought of his death *exclusively* in terms of Isa. 53 (Zech. 9.9 ff and 13.7 [Mark 11 1-10 and 14.27 respectively] have also played some part in his thinking, as well as certain Psalms) but we do maintain that this was the dominant passage of scripture in his mind, and that it is this passage which gives a remarkable unity to all his utterances about his death. Here then we have what Bultmann has failed to offer us: an intelligible, consistent explanation of the death of Jesus, and one which stands in organic relation with his proclamation: 'The Kingdom of God is at hand.'

IV

THE RAW MATERIALS
OF CHRISTOLOGY

WE have reached the conclusion that Bultmann's reconstruction of the history of Jesus is, to say the least, inadequate. Jesus was not only the prophet of the imminent advent of the eschatological Reign of God, but he also conceived it to be his mission to provide by his death the decisive occasion through and in which God would inaugurate that event whose imminence was the burden of his proclamation. This conclusion has been reached without directly raising the question whether Jesus claimed to be the Messiah or possessed a 'Messianic consciousness'. That is as it should be, for Jesus did not come in the first instance to teach a doctrine about his person, but to perform a particular historical task. The decision about his person arises from the decision about him as event, from the decision about what God is performing in him.[1] Nor must we expect that Jesus directly taught anything in the nature of a 'Christology'. What we have to look for is rather in the nature of presuppositions and hints which arise from his interpretation of his destiny. If Jesus betrayed such presuppositions or dropped any hints about his person, we may expect that those presuppositions will be consonant with his interpretation of his mission as we have established it thus far. They will express his conviction that his mission was to proclaim the impending advent of the eschatological Reign of God and to perform the event through which that Reign would be inaugurated. In other words, Jesus' presuppositions about his person will express both his present activity during his historical life, and that destiny which will be achieved in the future as the outcome of that history. Of course, these presuppositions are not proclaimed from the house-tops. They are hinted

---

[1] Cf. John 14.10-11, where it is expressly stated that the response of faith in the person of Jesus proceeds from a decision about his *works*.

only in the interpretation of his mission and destiny which he gave in private discourse with his closest disciples. Jesus provides the raw materials for an estimate of his person only for those who will later know what to do with them, only to those who have already shown themselves as men with eyes to see and ears to hear, however indistinctly, something of what God is doing in him. Here, as elsewhere, it is true that 'to him that hath shall be given'.

We proceed now to analyse the part played in the teaching of Jesus of this 'raw material for Christology'. We are led to the consideration of five different conceptions: (1) The Son of God, (2) The Servant, (3) The Son of Man, (4) The Christos, (5) The Kyrios, (6) The Son of David.

I. THE SON OF GOD

It is Bultmann's opinion that the term 'Son of God' was first applied to Jesus after the Resurrection by the earliest Aramaic-speaking Church.[1] This Church believed that Jesus was not the Messiah in his earthly life, but that God had instituted him as such only after the Resurrection. So, taking its cue from Ps. 2.7 ('Thou art my Son, this day have I begotten thee') it applied the title 'Son of God' to Jesus in his *exalted* state. This stage of development has been reached in the Transfiguration story, which, as we have seen, Bultmann thinks was originally a Resurrection narrative. Later, when Christianity was transferred to an Hellenistic environment, the term Son of God acquired two wider associations, first that of the Hellenistic divine man (θεῖος ἀνήρ) who by his startling exploits proved himself to be of supernatural origin, and secondly that of the gnostic Redeemer, pre-existent in eternity, manifested on earth, and returning to heaven again. Thus the way was open for a reading back of the Sonship of Jesus into his earthly life; the Transfiguration narrative could be pressed back into the earthly life of Jesus, and the 'legends' of the Baptism and the Q version of the Temptation constructed. However startling this may seem to the English reader, it should be

[1] *Theology*, p. 28, p. 32.

observed that this position does at least represent an important advance on Bousset. For Bultmann admits, as Bousset does not,[1] that it was not the Hellenistic Church which first applied 'Son of God' to Jesus, but the Aramaic-speaking Church, and therefore that, *when first introduced*, its meaning was not Hellenistic, but Hebraic. It is, however, uncertain whether Ps. 2.7 can bear the weight which Bultmann places upon it, and his argument seems to be weakened by the apparent rarity of the use of 'Son of God' as a Messianic title in contemporary Judaism, a rarity of which he is not unaware.[2] It is quite true, as Bultmann states, that the earliest Church applied Ps. 2.7 to Jesus in reference to his exaltation, but it is not equally clear that the origin of the Synoptic use of Son of God as applied to Jesus in his earthly life was that which Bultmann suggests. For Rom. 1.4 asserts that at the Resurrection Jesus was 'defined as Son of God *with power*' (ὁρισθέντος υἱοῦ θεοῦ ἐν δυνάμει.). Now this seems to imply that even the pre-Pauline Church knew that already in his earthly life Jesus was 'Son of God' in some other sense than 'in power', viz., in weakness and humiliation. This raises the possibility that the Synoptic application of 'Son of God' to Jesus was derived neither from Ps. 2.7 and Jewish Messianism (as Bultmann supposes in the case of the Transfiguration) nor from Hellenistic religiosity (as Bultmann assumes in the case of the Baptism and the Q version of the Temptation). It is hard, moreover, to see why Bultmann posits a different origin for the use of 'Son of God' in the Baptism narrative from that in the Transfiguration. In both cases the background of the pronouncement of the heavenly Voice is neither Ps. 2.7[3] nor Hellenism, but Isa. 42.1 ff.[4] And in the case of the Q version of the Temptation the idea of

[1] *Kyrios Christos*, 1921, pp. 52 ff. Cf. Rawlinson, *Christ*, p. 42, footnote 6.
[2] *Theology*, p. 50. In the late Jewish Apocalyptic literature the designation 'Son of God' occurs in the book of Enoch only at 105.2, but Enoch 105 is lacking in the Greek text (*Chester Beatty Papyrus*, ed. C. Bonner); cf. J. Bieneck, *Sohn Gottes*, 1951, pp. 24 f). It occurs in 2 Esdras (7.28 f; 13.32, 37, 52; 14.9) but 2 Esdras can hardly be the source of Christian usage, since it dates only from the end of the first century A.D. Mark 14.61 is a possible instance of pre-Christian Jewish use, but Luke 22.67 may preserve the original wording of the High Priest's question.
[3] For a discussion of the variant reading found at Luke 3.22, see below p. 86 f.
[4] See pp. 53 f, 87 f.

F

The Mission and Achievement of Jesus

Sonship is based firmly upon the Sonship of Israel in the wilderness, for Jesus grounds his interpretation of the divine Sonship on texts derived from Deuteronomy.[1] Not only is the derivation palpably different from what Bultmann suggests; the meaning of 'Son of God' in the Temptation narrative is wholly incompatible with its supposed derivation from Hellenistic sources. For the θεῖος ἀνήρ was pre-eminently one who called attention to his supernatural character by his wonderful deeds, whereas by quoting from Deuteronomy Jesus rejects precisely this as a diabolical temptation. Clearly then we have every right to look for a different origin and background to the application by the Synoptic Gospels of the title 'Son of God' to Jesus during his earthly life.

Now it will hardly be doubted that, quite apart from what we may or may not know about the 'religious experience' of Jesus (and the form critics are right enough in their insistence that we know very little), the recorded sayings of Jesus in the Gospels suggest that he called God his Father in a new and unique way. In Mark 14.36 we are told that Jesus addressed God in Aramaic as 'Abba'. Now although the Gethsemane prayer is quite possibly the composition of the Church, since the only possible witnesses were seemingly out of ear-shot, and for part of the time at any rate asleep, it is clear that the Gethsemane tradition as a whole has been constructed from the indubitably authentic teaching of Jesus in the Lord's Prayer.[2] Now in Luke 11.2 the address is simply πατέρ (= Abba), and Matthew's addition (6.9) of ἡμῶν ὁ ἐν τοῖς οὐρανοῖς is undoubtedly secondary.[3] Moreover the continued liturgical use of the Aramaic word 'Abba' even in Greek-speaking circles suggests that there was something peculiar about it. Now the Aramaic-speaking Jew addressed God as 'ābbi, 'my Father' and his earthly progenitor as 'abbā', 'father'.[4] The inference is that 'Abba', like the English vocative 'father', suggests a familiarity incompatible with the Jew's relationship to God.

[1] Matt. 4.4=Luke 4.4 from Deut. 8.3; Matt. 4.7=Luke 4.12 from Deut. 6.16; Matt. 4.10=Luke 4.8 from Deut. 6.13.
[2] Cf. 'Abba', Mark 14.36 with 'Father', Luke 11.2: 'not what I will but thou wilt' with 'thy will be done', Matt. 6.10; cf. also 'temptation' in Mark 14.38.
[3] Cf. his addition of μού to Mark's πατέρ at 26.39, 42.
[4] For evidence see G. Kittel, T.W.N.T., I, pp. 4 ff.

82

Jesus however boldly addresses God as Abba, and as Dalman has said, it is 'the homely language of the child to his father'.[1] This might lead us to suppose that Jesus regarded himself as the Son of God in a correspondingly unique sense. But the evidence for the use by Jesus of 'Son of God' as a self-designation is meagre in the extreme. In the parable of the Vineyard (Mark 12.6) God sends his υἱὸς ἀγαπητός as the culmination of redemptive history. Jesus does not explicitly identify that figure with himself. No doubt the identification is implied, but it is a simile, rather than a direct claim. In Mark 13.32 Jesus disclaims any knowledge on the part of 'the Son' as to the date of the End. In view of the 'scandalous' nature of this saying—Luke omits the whole verse (see his parallel at 21.33) and many MSS. of Matthew, more frequently used in church than Mark, also omit οὐδὲ ὁ υἱός—it is most unlikely that the verse is a Christian addition to a Jewish apocalypse.[2] On the other hand the context suggests that by the Son is meant, not Jesus himself in his earthly existence, but the heavenly Son of Man (whatever the relation between the Son of Man and the earthly Jesus may be, a subject which we leave over for the present), and indeed, the 'Trinitarian' formula, Father, Son, and angels, suggests that the original form may have been God, Son of Man, angels.[3] Hence we cannot use this passage as certain evidence for our Lord's conception of his Sonship during his earthly life. Apart from these two passages, the term Son of God is applied to Jesus only by others: by the Evangelist himself, if this reading at Mark 1.1 be correct, by the Voice from Heaven at the Baptism and Transfiguration (Mark 1.11, 9.7 ὁ υἱός μου ὁ ἀγαπητός, as in 12.6), by the demons (3.11, 5.7), by the High Priest at Mark 14.61 (ὁ υἱὸς τοῦ εὐλογητοῦ, apparently there as the equivalent of Χριστός: the Lukan version (22.26) is probably more original at this point); and lastly by the centurion at the cross (Mark 15.39). Nor, when we turn to the Q material is the situation any different. The term 'Son'

---

[1] cited Kittel, *ibid.*
[2] So Bultmann, *Tradition*, p. 130.
[3] Cf. Mark 8.38, and the rudiments of an 'Apocalyptic Trinity' of this kind in Enoch 39.5-7, 51.3 f, 61.8-10. See Ernst Lohmeyer in : *In Memoriam Ernst Lohmeyer*, pp. 30 f.

is applied to Jesus by himself only in the notorious 'Synoptic thunderbolt from the Johannine sky' at Matt. 11.27 para., a passage whose authenticity is so much in doubt that we cannot use it to prove anything.[1] It also is put into the mouth of the devil in the Temptation narrative at Matt. 4.3, 6 para. Clearly the situation is not very encouraging. On the other hand it must be remembered that, as we have already remarked, Jesus did not come to teach a Christology or doctrine about his person, but to perform a mission, and it is not therefore surprising that there is not a single passage where he directly claims to be the Son of God. That indeed seems to be the historical truth. Jesus did not 'claim' to be the Son of God, or directly call himself such, but he did know that he stood in a unique relationship of Sonship to God. It is here that the importance of the Baptism, Temptation and Transfiguration lies. It is unnecessarily sceptical to deny that the stories of the Baptism and Temptation (Q version) go back to Jesus himself. We know that he spoke on more than one occasion of John the Baptist, and associated his own authority with his Baptism by John (Matt. 11.7 ff para.; Mark 11.30 ff). We know also that the subject of πειρασμός was one on which he spoke to his disciples (Matt. 6.13 para.; Mark 14.38; Luke 22.28). What is more likely than that Jesus explained to his disciples that the basis of his authority was that unique Sonship which the encounter of his Baptism made explicit, and that his awareness of this unique Sonship was precisely the ground of his temptations? It does not seem to be unreasonable then to conclude that Jesus knew himself to be the υἱὸς τοῦ θεοῦ, the Son of God in a unique sense, although this is a status which he would never directly claim: it is the Voice from Heaven which proclaims him as such, not a claim of his own. It is the devil and the evil spirits, and finally the high priest and the centurion, who use this designation. For Sonship means to Jesus not a dignity to be claimed, but a responsibility to be fulfilled. This presence of a unique Sonship in the recorded history of Jesus is not to be rejected because it is Messianic, and therefore post-Resurrection. During the actual history of Jesus it is rather

[1] See however below, pp. 89 ff.

pre-Messianic. It is a relationship on the basis of which Jesus
will perform the work which will lead men later to confess
that God has exalted him as the Messiah. Jesus is not the Son
because he is the Messiah, and therefore both Son and Messiah
only after his Resurrection, as Bultmann maintains. He enters
upon the dignity of the Messiah after his Resurrection, because
during his earthly life he was the Son. The Son-hood is the
basis of his Messiahship, not the Messiahship the basis of his
Son-hood.

Now to the Hebrew mind the father-son relationship meant
far more than a statement of physical origin. It connoted
favour and care on the part of the father, and the response of
filial love, authority on the one side, and obedience on the
other.[1] In particular, by obedient submission to the father's
will, the son becomes a perfect reproduction of his father at
every point. When Jesus calls God his Father in a unique
sense, and by implication himself the unique Son, he is not
making a Messianic, still less a metaphysical or a mystical
statement. Neither Jewish Messianism, nor Hellenistic mythology, nor Nicene metaphysics, nor the modern idea of a unique
religious experience gives the clue to the Sonship of Jesus as
he himself understood it. The Father-Son relationship in
which Jesus knew himself to stand is a relationship involving
choice and response, authority and obedience. The basic
pattern for this relationship is to be found in the Sonship of
Israel in the Old Testament.

> Israel is my son, my firstborn: and I have said unto thee,
> Let my son go, that he may serve me (Ex. 4.22b-23a).
> When Israel was a child, then I loved him, and called my
> son out of Egypt (Hos. 11.1).

Israel is constituted the Son by the choice of God in the events
of the Exodus, and for Israel it involves the response on her
side of filial love and obedience. That this formed the pattern
of Jesus' own Sonship is suggested in the Q account of the
Temptation, in which as we have seen[2] Jesus answers the devil
out of Deuteronomy. Sonship means for Jesus what it was

[1] Cf. T. W. Manson, *Teaching*, pp. 89 ff.   [2] above p. 82, footnote 1.

intended to mean for Israel, the unquestioning response to the event of God's choice by unswerving obedience to his will. But while the Israel of the Old Covenant provides the pattern of choice and obedience, the choice and obedience of Jesus are unique, for they are set in a unique context. The mission of Jesus is not simply the mission of Israel, to obey the Torah as such. It is rather a unique mission of choice and obedience in relation to the *eschatological will* of God, the choice and response of one who, as we have seen in the two previous chapters, was to proclaim the imminent advent of the Reign of God, and to perform the event in and through which God would set it in motion. It is not surprising therefore to find that the language of Sonship is qualified by the Servant language from Deutero-Isaiah. The one in fact merges into the other.

2. THE SERVANT

As we have already seen, Bultmann's contention that the Servant language appears only in the later strata of the New Testament is unfounded. It is a doctrine which belongs precisely to the earliest Aramaic stratum of the New Testament.[1] Indeed it has a high claim to represent our Lord's own conception of his mission. At this point our concern is to show how it is related to and serves to qualify the language of Sonship. To do this we must begin with the Voice from Heaven at Jesus' Baptism:

Mark 1.11	Matt. 3.17	Luke 3.22
σὺ εἶ ὁ υἱός μου ὁ ἀγαπητός, ἐν σοὶ εὐδόκησα	οὗτός ἐστιν ὁ υἱός μου ὁ ἀγαπητός, ἐν ᾧ εὐδόκησα	σὺ εἶ ὁ υἱός μου ὁ ἀγαπητός, ἐν σοὶ ηὐδόκησα [2]v.l.: υἱός μου εἶ σύ, ἐγὼ σήμερον γεγέννηκά σε.

Earlier in this century, most scholars accepted the Western reading as original to Luke (and Q).[3] Most recent critics,[4]

[1] See above, p. 54.
[2] Most Western texts: *D a b c* ff[2]; also Iren., Justin, Clem. Alex., Origen, Hilary.
[3] e.g. Harnack, *Sayings*, pp. 310-314; Streeter, *Four Gospels*, 1924, pp. 143, 276; Klostermann, *Luke, ad loc.*; V. Taylor, *Behind the Third Gospel*, 1925, p. 77, cf. 145n.
[4] Easton, Creed and Rengstorf, *Luke, ad loc.*

though not all,[1] argue in favour of the traditional reading. In addition to the arguments, both external and intrinsic, which have been advanced by these scholars, it is to be noted that the citation of Ps. 2 in this context is most inappropriate. For the Voice from Heaven is intended as the scriptural interpretation of the significance of the descent of the Spirit upon Jesus. Now in Ps. 2 not a word is said of the Son's endowment with the Spirit. Indeed, the Son of Ps. 2 is a wholly different character. So far from being endowed with the Spirit to proclaim good tidings to the poor (cf. Luke 4.18), he is described as one who will 'break his enemies with a rod of iron, and dash them in pieces like a potter's vessel' (Ps. 2.9). No wonder that the early Church associated this Psalm with the *exaltation* of Christ (Acts 13.33; Heb. 1.5, 5.5; cf. Rev. 2.27, 12.5, 19.15) rather than with his earthly life. It seems therefore most unlikely that Luke should have deliberately set aside his Markan exemplar in favour of such an inappropriate quotation from Ps. 2. The more probable explanation of the Western reading is that it is due to assimilation to the text of the LXX.[2] We may therefore examine the Markan text of the Voice from Heaven with complete confidence. Now it is usually regarded as a mixed quotation from Ps. 2.7 and Isa. 42.1.[3] Jeremias on the other hand[4] contends that υἱός represents an original παῖς = 'ĕbĕdh, thus restricting the quotation exclusively to Isa. 42.1. It may however be suggested that we have here something far more profound than either of these interpretations suggest. *Fundamental* to the Voice from Heaven is neither Ps. 2 nor Isa. 42, but the 'unique' Sonship of Jesus (υἱός ἀγαπητός),[5] unique in the sense that in the purpose of God he was called to perform the unique mission of proclaiming the imminent advent of the coming Reign, perform its signs, and accomplish the unique event through which God would actually inaugurate his Reign.

---

[1] See C. H. Turner, J.T.S. XVII, pp. 113 ff; Schrenk, T.W.N.T., II, p. 738, footnote 7.

[2] Cf. J. Jeremias, T.W.N.T., V, p. 699, who remarks that assimilations of this kind are characteristic of the Western text.

[3] See e.g. Rawlinson and Taylor, *Mark, ad loc.*; Lampe, *Seal*, p. 37. Dr. Taylor, however, regards it not as direct citation, but as a recollection of a number of O.T. passages, including the two texts mentioned above. [4] T.W.N.T., V, p. 699.

[5] See C. H. Turner, J.T.S. XVII, pp. 113 ff; Schrenk, T.W.N.T., p. II, 738, footnote 7.

This unique Sonship is not inaugurated by the Voice from Heaven: it is *presupposed and defined* by it (by reference to Isa. 42), directed and canalized along the lines of the fulfilment of the destiny of the Spirit-endowed Servant in proclamation and signs, in suffering and death.

Now it is often asserted that the Markan narrative of the Baptism must be read simply as the kerygmatic witness of the Church, not as an historical report of Jesus' own interpretation of his person. In particular, we are told, the account must not be interpreted as an 'experience' of Jesus. It is true that Mark gives us not an 'experience' but a transcendental event. Now the historian *qua* historian cannot deal with a transcendental event. But he can surely say that an event occurred, the precise this-worldly nature of which he cannot from the evidence reconstruct, but which was certainly an event which its recipient recognized as a transcendental encounter. The narrative of Acts for instance relates the conversion of Paul on the road to Damascus in terms of a Heavenly Voice and a light from heaven (Acts 9.3-8, 22.6-11, 26.12-18). This is presented as a transcendental event, which as such is beyond the ken of the historian. Acts does not give any clue for the reconstruction of Paul's 'experience'. Yet the historian cannot deny that an event did take place, and that Paul himself interpreted this event as a transcendental encounter (Gal. 1.15; I Cor. 15.8). There would seem to be no valid reason why the Baptism narrative should not be regarded in the same light. The historian cannot reconstruct the 'experience' of Jesus, for the narrative in Mark gives us a transcendental encounter. He cannot, *qua* historian, decide whether what did occur was actually a transcendental encounter. But he can surely affirm that an encounter did occur which Jesus himself, and not merely the Church, interpreted as a transcendental encounter, which pointed him to a fulfilment of a unique Sonship along the lines of Isa. 42. In postulating this, the historian is not going one whit further than what has already been established in Chapters II and III about the proclamation, signs, and death of Jesus. We conclude then that Jesus taught his disciples that he himself stood in a unique relation of Sonship to God, and that this Sonship was to find the essential pattern of its obedience in the fulfilment of the destiny of the Isaianic Servant.

At this point it will be pertinent to pay some attention to the so-called 'Synoptic thunderbolt from the Johannine sky' (Matt. 11.27=Luke 10.22). It will be remembered that we deliberately left it out of account as evidence to support our thesis that Jesus understood himself to be the Son of God in a unique sense, since its genuineness is so widely questioned. This need not however prevent us from examining the passage to see whether it is patient of an interpretation within the limits of the self-understanding of Jesus as we have established it thus far.

In Matthew the saying occurs as the second of three strophes:

Strophe I: Matt. 11.25-26 (=Luke 10.21)

I thank thee, O Father, Lord of heaven and earth, that thou didst hide these things from the wise and understanding, and didst reveal them unto babes: yea, Father, for so it was well-pleasing in thy sight.

Strophe II: Matt. 11.27 (=Luke 10.22)

All things have been delivered unto me of my Father: and *no one knoweth the Son, save the Father;* neither doth any know the Father, save the Son, and he to whomsoever the Son willeth to reveal him.

Strophe III: Matt. 11.28-30 (om. Luke)

Come unto me, all ye that labour and are heavy laden, and I will give you rest.
Take my yoke upon you, and learn of me;
for I am meek and lowly in heart;
and ye shall find rest unto your souls.
For my yoke is easy, and my burden is light.

W. Manson[1] gives a useful account of the treatment of this passage, which may be supplemented by Bieneck.[2] Briefly the position is as follows: Critics of the History of Religions

[1] *Messiah*, pp. 71 ff.
[2] *Sohn Gottes* pp. 75-87.

School[1] and their successors the form critics,[2] agree that Strophe II is a product of Hellenistic Christianity, and betrays the influence of gnosticism and the mystery religions. Strophe III is regarded by these critics for the most part as a Jewish (not Hellenistic) wisdom logion which has been transferred to Jesus. Strophe I alone is considered to be possibly authentic. A mediating position was adopted by Harnack, who writing before the advent of the History of Religions School[3] argued for the originality of all three Strophes, save for the italicized clause in Strophe II, which on the ground of certain second-century patristic evidence he rejected as a later interpolation. In this country the tendency has been to welcome Harnack as an ally against the form critics and their predecessors.[4] Recent attempts have been made however on the Continent to rescue all three Strophes of the Matthean version.[5] Bieneck's arguments are particularly worthy of attention. He begins by pointing out that the radical critics have no real reason for jettisoning the whole of Strophe II, except their unproven and over-hasty assumption that it must necessarily reflect the ideas of gnosticism and the mystery religions. A safer procedure is to try first to see whether we can make sense of it within the framework of the known history of Jesus. Secondly, Bieneck argues that Harnack's rejection of the italicized clause in Strophe II is equally unfounded.[6] Thirdly, following up a hint of Dibelius,[7] he argues that Luke's omission of Strophe III is due, not to its absence from Q, but to the fact that it is inappropriate to his context (the return of the Seventy). In view therefore of these recent attempts to rehabilitate the passage, we may feel some degree of confidence in taking the Matthean

[1] W. Bousset, *Kyrios Christos*, pp. 45 ff; Klostermann, *Matthew*, pp. 101 ff; E. Norden, *Agnostos Theos*, 1913, pp. 277 ff; Jackson and Lake, *Beginnings*, I, pp. 395 f.

[2] Bultmann, *Tradition*, p. 171, etc., *Gnosis*, 1952, pp. 50 f; Dibelius, *Tradition*, pp. 279-383; Kümmel, *Verheissung*, pp. 34 f.

[3] *Sayings*, pp. 272-310.

[4] e.g. W. Manson, *loc. cit.*

[5] Schlatter, *Matthew, ad loc.*; Schniewind, *Matthew, ad loc.*; Bieneck, *Sohn Gottes*, pp. 82-87.

[6] Dom. W. Chapman, in a trenchant critique of Harnack's theory (J.T.S., X, pp. 552 ff) had already shown that the textual variations in the Fathers are almost certainly due to quotation from memory.

[7] *Tradition*, p. 279, footnote 2.

version as it stands, not necessarily as giving us *ipsissima verba* of Jesus, but at least as representing an early tradition about him, since it occurs in Q. We shall therefore endeavour to make sense of the passage without recourse to textual excisions after the manner of Harnack, or to gnostic or mystery hypotheses like the historians of religion or the form critics.

We begin with an examination of the central and crucial Strophe II, since the interpretation of this will determine the interpretation of Strophes I and III.

(i) *'All things are delivered unto me of my Father'*

The aorist tense παρεδόθη, 'were delivered', requires a specific event between the Father and the Son. There are two possibilities: either it refers to the exaltation of Jesus after his death (cf. ἐδόθη μοι πᾶσα ἐξουσία, Matt. 28.18), in which case this will be a saying of the exalted Christ transferred to the historical Jesus (cf. Matt. 18.20); or it refers to the Baptism of Jesus, in which case it may be taken as a saying of the historical Jesus. The historical associations of the verb 'to know' in the following clause[1] would appear to favour the second possibility. In that case the πάντα will be the Reign of God which Jesus is to proclaim and inaugurate by fulfilling the mission of the Servant.

(ii) *'And no one knoweth ((ἐπι) γινώσκει) the Son save the Father'*

Two textual questions must be dealt with first. There is some early patristic evidence for ἔγνω instead of (ἐπι) γιγνώσκει, and Harnack strongly favoured this reading, as representing what *Luke* found in Q.[2] Dom Chapman[3] however conclusively demonstrated that the patristic quotations with ἔγνω are from *Matthew*, not Luke, and plausibly argued that the use of the aorist tense was due to quotation from memory and implied no essential difference of meaning. There is no need, therefore, to suppose with Bieneck[4] that ἔγνω is an adoptionist emendation, though we may safely assume that (ἐπι) γινώσκει is the original reading of Q. The second textual problem is that Luke

---

[1] See below.   [2] *Sayings*, pp. 282 ff.
[3] *Loc. cit.*   [4] *Ibid.*

has 'who the Son is' and 'who the Father is' after the verb γινώσκει. The effect of this version is to reduce the meaning of 'know' to its ordinary secular significance, 'to be cognisant of a fact', in this case the identity of the Son and the Father. Luke's version is an attempt to improve the Greek at the expense of theological profundity, and we may assume that Matthew correctly reproduces the original version of Q. What is meant by 'the Father knoweth the Son'? For an answer we must go to the Old Testament use of the verb *yādhā'* which is rendered in the LXX indifferently by γινώσκειν and εἰδέναι. When God 'knows' a man, it means that he has by a concrete event chosen him for a specific task in relation to his redemptive purpose in history, and continues to make him the object of his loving care as he executes the task to which he has been called. Primarily, God's people Israel is the object of his knowledge: 'You only have I known of all the families of the earth' (Amos 3.2). God's knowledge of Israel was actualized in the event of the Exodus: 'I did know thee in the wilderness' (Hos. 13.5). It may also be used of individuals who have a specific task in relation to the sacred history of God with his people. Thus Moses can say of himself, addressing Yahweh: 'Yet thou hast said, I know thee by name, and thou hast also found grace in my sight' (Ex. 33.12), while Jeremiah tells us how the Word of the Lord came to him, saying: 'Before I formed thee in the belly I knew thee' (Jer. 1.5). Thus we have a clear Old Testament background for the understanding of our Q logion. The Father's 'knowledge' of the Son consists in the choice of him to fulfil the role of the Servant, initiated in the Voice from Heaven at the Baptism of Jesus (ἐν σοὶ εὐδόκησα, Mark 1.11 para.; Isa. 42.1), and continued in the Father's loving care of his Son throughout his ministry. Again the Son's mission depends solely on the authorization of the Father: 'No one knoweth the Son.' The rejection of Jesus by the 'wise and understanding' (Matt. 11.25) does not throw the slightest shadow of doubt on the mission of the Son as the Servant of God; in fact it confirms his mission, for to be despised and rejected and disesteemed is precisely the function of the Servant (Isa. 53.3).

The Raw Materials of Christology

(iii) *'Neither doth any know the Father, save the Son'*

To know God, in the language of the Old Testament, is not to have some esoteric religious experience or *gnosis*, but to be the object of the divine choice and to respond to that choice in faith and obedience.[1] It is significant that the Old Testament repeatedly complains that Israel did *not* know God, for it constantly disobeyed his will (Isa. 1.3; Jer. 2.8; cf. 8.7). Hence the knowledge of God is eventually relegated to the eschatological hope (Jer. 31.34). It is this eschatological knowledge which Jesus, as the Son, enjoys, and which he is through his proclamation and activity revealing to other men, as the fourth clause of the verse asserts:

(iv) *'And he to whomsoever the Son willeth to reveal him'*

There is no reason to suppose that Jesus is here presented as a Hellenistic mystagogue, who mediates an esoteric *gnosis* to the initiate. We are still moving within the framework of Old Testament eschatology. For the idea is already present in Isa. 53.11: 'by his knowledge shall my righteous servant justify many.' And again, 'knowledge' is one of the endowments of the Son of David in Isa. 11.2 (a figure which Jesus possibly identified with the servant of Chapters 42 and 53).[2] The 'knowledge', then, which Jesus mediates, is the proclamation of the impending advent of the eschatological Reign of God, in which the powers of that Reign are already proleptically at work in him. 'Jesus speaks of the apprehension of the divine activity, as it is happening in the present and becoming history.'[3] Thus we cannot agree with the critics of the History of Religions School that we have strayed here into some Hellenistic sphere in which we have lost all contact with the Jesus of History. Nor does Harnack's omission of the italicized clause really help matters, since it ruins the theology of the whole passage. For it is the Father's knowledge of the Son, his choice and election of Jesus to fulfil the role of the Suffering Servant, which is the sole ground of the Son's knowledge of the Father,

[1] See Bultmann in T.W.N.T., I, pp. 696 ff. Eng. trans. *Gnosis*, pp. 15-18. Bultmann however does not make use of his findings for the understanding of Matt. 11.27, which he regards as Hellenistic.
[2] See below, p. 115.   [3] Schlatter, *Matthew*, ad loc.

93

that is, his obedient fulfilment of his destined role. Without his prior knowledge by the Father, the Son's claim to know him becomes an unsupportable act of arrogance. As Sir Edwyn Hoskyns has written in another connexion[1]: 'Jesus is the Son of God, not because he as a man claimed to be so, but because God sent him into the world as his Son.'

There still remains Strophe III to be considered. Many critics[2] have quite rightly called attention to the affinities between this Strophe and Ecclus. 51.23-26. What has not been noticed sufficiently however is the mixed character of the Strophe. It has a double background, partly in Ecclus. 51, but partly also in the later chapters of Isaiah. The self-description of Jesus as 'meek' and 'lowly' echoes the description of the Servant in Isa. 42.2-3 and 53.1 ff, while the invitation 'come unto me' recalls the invitation of Isa. 55.1-3. It looks as though we have the same blending of a 'Wisdom' Christology (here in a very rudimentary form) with the Sonship of Jesus conceived in terms of the obedient Servant, such as we find in a more developed form in the Fourth Gospel. For the Jesus of the Fourth Gospel is at once the pre-existent Logos or Wisdom of God (John 1.1-14) and the Son, whose Sonship is expressed in obedience to the Father's will (John 4.34, 5.30, 6.38-40) as his Servant.[3]

Can we now come to any decision about the authenticity of the 'Synoptic thunderbolt'? So far as its *content* is concerned, there is nothing in it which is inconsistent with our Lord's own conception of his Sonship in his earthly life as we have established it thus far. There are however two difficulties with regard to the *form* in which the Sonship of Jesus is asserted. First, the Synoptic tradition elsewhere, in passages whose authenticity we have every reason to accept, is careful to present the divine Sonship of Jesus, not as a claim which he

[1] *The Fourth Gospel*, 1940, I, p. 91.   [2] See e.g. W. Manson, *Messiah*, p. 73.
[3] For the possibility that ὁ ἀμνὸς τοῦ θεοῦ in John 1.29 and 33 represents Aramaic *ṭālya' dhēlāhā'* which=both 'lamb of God' and 'servant of God'; see C. F. Burney, *The Aramaic Origin of the Fourth Gospel*, 1922, pp. 107 f. This has been disputed, but the Isaianic background to John 1.29, 33 still stands. For a similar blending of Wisdom and Servant Christology cf. Oxyrhynchus Papyrus I, saying 3, discussed by Jeremias, *Jesusworte*, p. 66. The affinities between the Servant and Wisdom conceptions may have been suggested already by Isa. 11.2.

made for himself, but as a dignity acknowledged by the Father in the Voice from Heaven. In this passage however, Jesus directly calls himself the Son. Secondly, there are according to Dalman[1] linguistic difficulties in the absolute use of 'Son' in Aramaic. In view of these considerations, one hesitates to pronounce a decisive verdict on the historicity of this logion. But it is the product of a Christianity which has remained in very close touch with the mind of the historical Jesus: its conception of Sonship is his own, not the Hellenistic conception of the gnostic Redeemer. In this way, perhaps, the logion forms a bridge between the Synoptic Jesus and the Jesus of the Fourth Gospel.[2] For the Jesus of the Fourth Gospel is made the mouthpiece of the Church's faith, yet that faith, we should maintain, is expressed in terms not Hellenistic, but Hebraic and biblical, and employs the raw materials which Jesus himself had provided.

To sum up then it would seem that while Jesus did not 'claim' to be the Son of God, his words presume the knowledge that he was the Son of God in the sense that he existed in a unique relationship with the Father which found its pattern in the Sonship of Israel in the Old Testament, and which therefore was expressed in terms of choice and care on the one hand, and of obedience on the other. Moreover, this obedience was to find its expression quite concretely in the fulfilment of the role of the Isaianic Servant, so that the proclamation, signs and passion should become the historical media in and through which the eschatological act of God was to be accomplished in history.

3. THE SON OF MAN

Much has been written and much discussion has taken place during the past fifty years about our Lord's use of the term 'Son of Man'.[3] It seems, however, that one result is at least

---

[1] *The Words of Jesus*, pp. 193 f.   [2] So J. Jeremias, *Jesusworte*, p. 65.

[3] For a convenient summary of the discussion up to 1926 see Rawlinson *Christ*, pp. 242 ff. Among more recent discussions in English we may note: T. W. Manson, *Teaching*, pp. 211-234; Otto, *Kingdom*, pp. 159-255; Taylor, *Sacrifice*, pp. 20-32; Flew, *Church*, pp. 74-6; C. J. Cadoux, *The Historic Mission of*

assured. Lietzmann's theory[1] that Jesus could never have used 'Son of Man' as a title, on the ground that in Aramaic *barnasha* means simply 'man', and that therefore the use of ὁ υἱὸς τοῦ ἀνθρώπου as a title originated in Hellenistic Christian circles, is now generally discarded. The term Son of Man, it is now generally agreed, was used as a title by Jesus himself. But at this point agreement ends.

It will be convenient at this point to have before us the three distinct groups into which the uses of the term 'Son of Man' fall in the Synoptic Gospels.

A. *Present Usage*

(i.e., those occurrences of 'Son of Man' where it is intended as a self-designation of Jesus present and active in his earthly ministry.)

Mark	Q	Special Matthew	Special Luke	Editorial
2.10	Matt. 8.20 = Luke 9.58	Matt. 13.37[2]	Luke 19.10	Matt. 16.13
2.28	Matt. 11.19 = Luke 7.34			Luke 6.22[3]
10.45[4]	Matt. 12.32 = Luke 12.10			

B. *'Suffering' Usage*

Mark	Q	Special Matthew	Special Luke	Editorial
8.31			Luke 22.22[5]	Matt. 26.2
9.12			Luke 24.7[5]	[Luke 17.25[6]]

Jesus, 1941, pp. 90-102; W. Manson, *Messiah*, pp. 113-120; G. S. Duncan, *Jesus Son of Man*, 1947, pp. 142-153; J. Y. Campbell, J. T. S., XLVIII, pp. 145 ff; art. 'Son of Man' in *Word Book*, pp. 230-232; Dodd, *Scriptures*, pp. 116 f. Briefly, English scholars are agreed that Jesus used the title of himself, but disagree as to the source from whence he derived it, and the sense in which he used it. Roughly, there are four possibilities: (i) Enochic-apocalyptic, fused with the Suffering Servant of Isaiah (Otto); (ii) Danielic-apocalyptic fused with the Servant (W. Manson, Taylor, Flew); (iii) Danielic-corporate (T. W. Manson, Cadoux); (iv) Ezekielic-prophetic (Campbell, Duncan).

[1] In: *Der Menschensohn*, 1896.

[2] The classification of this reference is difficult for two reasons: (i) It occurs in the allegorical interpretation of the parable of the Wheat and Tares, which may be either 'special Matthew' or editorial. (ii) There are two references to the Son of Man in the allegorical interpretation: the second reference is clearly 'future' (verse 41), but in this verse the sowing apparently refers to the activity of Jesus during his ministry.

[3] This may be from Q, but there is no Matthean parallel.

[4] This refers partly to the activity of Jesus in his ministry, but also contains, in the second half of the saying, an allusion to the Passion. It is therefore included among both the 'present' and the 'suffering' usages.

[5] Luke may have found this in his special source, but it may equally be an editorial modification of Mark.

[6] αὐτόν here refers to 'Son of man' in the previous verse. See p. 59, footnote 1.

Mark	*Q*	*Special Matthew*	*Special Luke*	*Editorial*
9.31				
10.33				
10.45				
14.21 *bis*)				
14.41				

C. *Future*

(i.e., those occurrences which clearly refer to the exalted and glorified Son of Man.)

Mark	*Q*	*Special Matthew*	*Special Luke*	*Editorial*
8.38	Matt. 12.40=Luke 11.30[2]	Matt. 10.23	Luke 17.22	Matt. 16.28
9.9[3]	Matt. 24.27=Luke 17.24	Matt. 13.41	Luke 17.30[4]	Matt. 24.30
13.26	Matt. 24.37=Luke 17.26	Matt. 19.28[5]	Luke 18.8	Luke 12.8[6]
14.62	Matt. 24.44=Luke 12.40	Matt. 24.39		
		Matt. 25.31		

Certain facts emerge from the foregoing table. (1) The 'present' and 'future' usages occur in both primary documents, Mark and Q. (2) The 'suffering' usage is confined to Mark (apart from three instances, one of which is editorial (Matt. 26.2), and the others quite possibly so (Luke 22.22, 24.7—see footnote 1 under B)). (3) The 'suffering' usage in Mark occurs in the prophecies of the Passion and in the Passion narrative only, never in combination with the 'future' usage. The 'future' sayings on the other hand never speak of suffering. From these facts Bultmann deduces certain conclusions[7]: (1)

---

[1] See footnote (4) under A.

[2] The wording of this saying in Matthew and Luke is very different, but it probably came originally from Q, in which case Luke probably preserves the original Q version, while Matthew's version is an editorial modification. In that case, the Q version was clearly a 'future' usage. In the Matthean form it refers to the burial of Jesus, and might therefore be included among the 'suffering' passages.

[3] Luke omits this saying. It is the only Son of Man saying associated *exclusively* with the Resurrection.

[4] Possibly Q, but there is no Matthean parallel.

[5] Streeter (*Four Gospels*, p. 288) assigns this verse to M. If however Luke 22.29 f was originally the same saying, it may have stood in Q. In that case Luke may preserve the original Q form, and Matthew's version, including the insertion of ὁ υἱὸς τοῦ ἀνθρώπου, will be editorial. On the other hand, the distinction between Jesus and the Son of Man suggests that the Matthean form may be more primitive (so Kümmel, *Verheissung*, p. 41).

[6] Possibly the phrase καὶ ὁ υἱὸς τοῦ ἀνθρώπου stood in Q; but Matthew has κἀγώ, and in view of his tendency to replace a simple ἐγώ by ὁ υἱὸς τοῦ ἀνθρώπου (cf. Matt. 16.13) it is unlikely that he adopted the reverse procedure here.

[7] *Theology*, pp. 30 ff.

G

Only the 'present' and the 'future' usages belong to the earlier strata of the tradition. (2) The 'suffering' usage is an invention of Mark, and its secondary character shown by the fact that it is not fused with the 'future' usage. (3) The 'present' usage Bultmann recognizes as authentic, but not as Messianic: it is simply the Aramaic periphrasis for 'man' or 'I'. (4) The 'future' usage is probably authentic to Jesus, and Messianic. But Jesus does not identify himself with the apocalyptic Son of Man: he merely announces his coming as one distinct from himself.

Now there are several questions here which call for consideration. First, what is the primary sense in which Jesus used the term Son of Man? An attempt has been made by some critics to turn the flank of Bultmann's position by denying that Jesus used the term in an apocalyptic sense at all,[1] but *invariably*[2] as a periphrasis for the first person singular. In other words, the first of the three usages, the 'present', is primary and normative for the others. One strong argument in favour of this thesis (as against Bultmann's view, which assumes that apart from usage A the apocalyptic-future use is primary and normative) is that the term 'Son of Man' does not appear to have been current as a Messianic title in pre-Christian Jewish apocalyptic. The only evidence that it was so used occurs in the Similitudes of Enoch (Enoch 37-70), and since these chapters have not appeared in any of the Greek fragments so far discovered, it is being increasingly suspected that they represent a Christian interpolation into the original Jewish text.[3] In favour of the authenticity of the Similitudes of Enoch it might perhaps be urged that the distinctively Christian feature of the Son of Man is lacking there, viz., his incarnate life and Passion: he is pre-existent and manifested at the End, that is all. But in any case, there is no reason to suppose that Jesus was familiar with the Similitudes of Enoch. We are left then with Dan. 7 and Ezek. 2.1, etc., as possible sources for Jesus'

---

[1] See p. 99, footnote 1.   [2] i.e. Not only in usage A, as Bultmann.

[3] Cf. Dodd, *Scriptures*, pp. 116 f. It is surprising that Bultmann, like other German scholars, e.g. E. Stauffer, *Die Theologie des neuen Testaments*, 1948⁴, p. 89 and footnote 317, still accepts the authenticity of the Ethiopian Enoch without question (*Theology*, p. 53).

use of 'Son of Man'. Daniel 7, however, it is argued, speaks not of *the* Son of Man (a title), but of 'one like unto a son of man' (i.e. a simile), and by it he means not an individual figure, but 'the saints of the Most High' (7.18, 22, 25, 27). Therefore Jesus cannot have derived his use of Son of Man from Daniel. Accordingly, we are left with Ezek. 2.1, etc. In this sense the term Son of Man 'suggests at once the littleness of the prophet as man, and the greatness to which God calls him in his service; through him, man though he is, God speaks to man, and carries out his high purposes'.[1] This argument, however, is open to three objections. In the first place it does not do justice to those very passages from which it claims to start, viz., the places where Jesus ostensibly identifies himself already during his ministry with the Son of Man. The Son of Man who dispenses eschatological forgiveness in Mark 2.10 is palpably more than one 'called to the service of God' in the sense that the prophet Ezekiel was called. Whether we can take this logion as an authentic saying of Jesus is a matter which will be discussed later,[2] but it is clear that Jesus is claiming here to be acting as one more than a prophet. He is acting as the one in whom the Kingdom of God, while it has not yet arrived, is nevertheless dawning.[3] 'Son of man' in Mark 2.10 must be given a weight and significance to correspond with Jesus' message of the coming Kingdom. It is not enough to say that he was just a prophet, and no more. The Ezekielic interpretation is inadequate. Still more inadequate is the theory that Jesus meant Son of Man in Mark 2.10 simply in the sense of 'man' or mankind. That interpretation reduces the saying to bathos, and indeed to blasphemy, as the opponents of Jesus rightly perceive. Jesus accepts the thesis of his enemies that God alone can forgive sins, but maintains that God is acting in himself and declaring in advance the eschatological forgiveness. Nevertheless, there may be an element of truth in the theory that 'Son of man' here is the equivalent of man or mankind. If the saying is authentic, Jesus' opponents would

[1] J. Y. Campbell in *Word Book*, pp. 231 f. Cf. the same, J.T.S., XLVIII. pp. 145 ff.
[2] See below, p. 106.   [3] See above, pp. 20 ff.

99

understand it in that sense, and could only so understand it (unless of course Son of Man was a current Messianic title, a theory which seems now to have been disproved). Perhaps then Jesus intended them to understand it in that sense, or at least he meant to conceal from them the deeper mystery attached to his person.[1] In that case the charge of blasphemy would in their eyes not have been refuted, but merely shelved —to be renewed at a later occasion.

The second instance of 'present' usage to be considered is the saying which concludes the episode of the Walking through the Cornfields: 'The Son of man is lord even of the sabbath' (Mark 2.28). It is attractive at first sight to interpret 'Son of man' here in the sense of 'mankind', man in general, particularly in view of verse 27: 'The sabbath was made for man, and not man for the sabbath.' But is it conceivable that Jesus would have taught that any man could do as he pleased with the Mosaic law? Elsewhere, Jesus dispenses with the Mosaic law of the Sabbath, not freely, or arbitrarily, but where the claims of the coming Kingdom are paramount and must therefore be accorded priority.[2] So in this story, the situation in which Jesus and his disciples find themselves, namely, in urgent expectation of the coming Kingdom, which is already breaking in, is an emergency situation comparable to that in which David took the shewbread. The emergency is created by the eschatological proclamation: only because Jesus is the Son of Man in an eschatological sense can he dispense with the law of the Sabbath. Hence the Ezekiel usage of the term 'son of man' is insufficient to bear the weight of this saying. There is also a possibility that the Sabbath was regarded already in Rabbinic Judaism as early as N.T. times as a type of the coming Messianic Kingdom,[3] but the evidence of the Mishnah cannot be dated with certainty earlier than the second century. Hoskyns[4] preferred to regard the interpretation of the Sabbath as the type of the coming Kingdom as a creative achievement made by

[1] See below, p. 106.
[2] Cf. references, on p. 71, footnote 1, also the story of the man working on the Sabbath in Codex D at Luke 6.5: 'Man, if thou knowest what thou doest, thou art blessed, but if thou knowest not, thou art accursed and a transgressor of the law.' [3] See E. C. Hoskyns in *Mysterium Christi*, p. 77. [4] *loc. cit.*

Jesus himself, whence it passed into early Christian theology (Heb. 4.10; John 5.17; Barn. 15). On the other hand, it is difficult to suppose that an interpretation of this kind could have arisen within Judaism *after* it had gained currency in Christian circles. If such an interpretation was already current within Judaism in our Lord's day it would give added point to his saying that the Son of Man is Lord of the Sabbath. It would also support our contention that the term 'Son of man' in this saying has an eschatological background which is inadequately accounted for on the supposition that its use is derived from Ezekiel.

The second objection against the Ezekiel hypothesis is that on the two occasions when Jesus refers explicitly to an Old Testament text (Mark 13.26 para., 14.62 para.), he recalls not Ezekiel, but Dan. 7.13.[1]

Thirdly, while the Ezekiel hypothesis may give a plausible, if defective, explanation of the sayings in group A, there are difficulties in applying it to the sayings in groups B and C. Although at first sight the sayings about the suffering Son of Man might be regarded as an extended use of the simple self-identification, there is nothing in Ezekiel's use of the term to warrant the assertion that the Son of Man 'must' suffer, or that it is 'written of him' that he should suffer. This again strongly suggests that the clue lies elsewhere. The same difficulty arises in an even more acute form with the Parousia sayings, particularly those where Jesus speaks of the Son of Man as a figure distinct from himself. The most striking example is Mark 8.38:

> For whosoever shall be ashamed of me and of my words in this . . . generation, the Son of man also shall be ashamed of him, when he cometh in the glory of his Father.[2]

Here a clear distinction is drawn between Jesus in his earthly ministry and the Son of Man to come. Indeed, as Bultmann rightly urges, none of the Parousia sayings explicitly identify

[1] Cf. Dalman, *The Words of Jesus*, pp. 257 ff; Dodd, *Scriptures*, p. 117, footnote 1, where the absence of Ezekiel among the primary sources of 'testimonies' is noted.
[2] Cf. also Matt. 19.28—see Group C, footnote 5.

Jesus with that Son of Man. Jesus' use of the term must have been far more complicated than any theory of simple self-identification would lead us to suppose.

It is clear then that we must seek the clue to Jesus' use of 'Son of Man' in the place where he himself apparently sought it, that is, in Dan. 7.[1] The common objection that Dan. 7.13 speaks not of 'the Son of Man', but simply of 'one like unto a son of man' is not decisive against its use as a title by Jesus. It may very well be that Jesus himself transformed Daniel's simile into a title for the glorified, supernatural bringer of salvation. Further, the objection that in Daniel the one like unto a son of man is not an individual figure, but 'the saints of the Most High', the glorified, eschatological Israel is not really an objection at all, but the strongest indication we have of the working of Jesus' mind. As we have already seen, Jesus conceived his own mission on earth in terms derived from the earthly history of Israel, i.e. in terms of Sonship. He individualized what was in the Old Testament a corporate conception. The same may apply also to his thinking about the Servant. In Deutero-Isaiah the term 'Servant' oscillates between a corporate and an individual conception. The Servant is primarily Israel, but as the true Israel it may be realized concretely in an individual figure. So Jesus conceives it his mission to embody this figure in his own person by his eschatological obedience as the true representative of Israel. May it not therefore be that Jesus took over the term 'Son of Man' and individualized it in precisely the same way? The 'saints of the Most High' become a concrete reality in the glorified figure who receives the eschatological Kingdom. What then is the relation between Jesus and the glorified Son of Man? That there is a distinction between them is shown by Mark 8.38, cf. Matt. 19.28. But that there is an organic connexion between Jesus and the Son of Man is also shown by the same texts. For it is a man's attitude to Jesus in his proclamation and activity in his earthly life, to Jesus as the sign and embodi-

[1] Ps. 8.4 and Ps. 80.17 have also been suggested as possible candidates (Dodd, *Scriptures*, p. 117). But Jesus does not use these Psalms in his recorded sayings, and it is difficult, though probably not impossible, to account for the detachment in the Parousia sayings between Jesus and the glorified Son of Man.

ment of the coming Kingdom, which determines a man's status before the glorified Son of Man, and determines whether a man will have a share in the Kingdom and glory of the Son of Man. Moreover, while Jesus frequently exhorts his followers to wait for the coming of the Son of Man[1] he never includes himself among those who are to wait. He stands as it were on the same side as the glorified Son of Man over against the disciples. Though Jesus is not to be identified in his ministry *tout court* with the coming Son of Man, he is closely associated with him. What then is the relation between them? I submit that it is identical with the relation between his ministry and the coming Kingdom. In the ministry of Jesus the Kingdom has not yet come, but is on its way and breaking in, proleptically active in his proclamation and healings. So also Jesus is not yet the glorified Son of Man. He has not yet been brought near to the ancient of days and received the everlasting dominion and the Kingdom that shall not be destroyed. Between Jesus and the fulfilment of Daniel's vision there stands the decisive event through which God is to inaugurate the Kingdom—the cross.

But what then of the suffering sayings and the 'present' usage of Son of Man, our groups A and B? Are we with Bultmann to reject the first as irrelevant and the second as unauthentic, because we cannot square them with our theory? By no means so. Let us take the suffering sayings first. 'The Son of man must suffer': 'The Son of man goeth as it is written of him.' That is to say, the suffering is the divinely ordained precondition for the coming of the glorified Son of Man. Jesus suffers not as the one who is already Son of Man, but as the one destined to be the Son of Man, as the Son of Man designate. That this was written in the scriptures precisely of the Son of Man, that the one destined to be the Son of Man must suffer, was Jesus' interpretation of the Son of Man as portrayed in the book of Daniel. Before Israel is glorified as the Son of Man and is given the dominion and power, the saints of the Most High suffer oppression at the hand of their enemies. Israel suffers in the persons of Shadrach,

[1] Mark 13.33-37; Luke 12.35-40; Matt. 24.42-51 para.

Meshach and Abednego in the burning fiery furnace of Dan. 3, in the person of Daniel himself in the lion's den of Chapter 6, and finally in the oppression of the four great beasts in Chapter 7, 3-8. The earthly sufferings of Israel are the prelude to Israel's inauguration as the triumphant Son of Man.[1] The use of Son of Man in the 'suffering' sense is perfectly compatible with what we have established about Jesus' conception of his mission; if, that is to say, he not only proclaimed the coming Kingdom, but conceived it to be his mission to perform the decisive act which would set it in motion. To say 'the Son of man must suffer' is not to utter a present-Messianic claim. It is to assert that by his sufferings Jesus will perform the event which lead to the triumph of the Kingdom of God. Nor are the literary difficulties raised by Bultmann against the authenticity of the sayings in group B decisive.[2] The absence of suffering Son of Man sayings from Q is partly accounted for by the fact that Q was not a gospel, and did not contain a Passion narrative. Hence the absence of Son of Man sayings such as those which occur in the heart of the Markan Passion narrative.[3] That there are no direct predictions of the Passion in Q, such as account for the remainder of the Markan Son of Man sayings in group B,[4] is also due to the fact that Q does not contain a Passion narrative. But although there are no direct predictions of the suffering of the Son of Man in Q, there is an indirect one:

The Son of man hath not where to lay his head (Matt. 8.20 = Luke 9.58).

This saying was classified under group A, to which it ostensibly belongs, but the question arises whether it should rather be assigned to group B (suffering sayings).[5] As in similar

---

[1] Cf. Dodd, *Scriptures*, p. 117: 'To say, as is often said, that the Old Testament knows nothing of a suffering Son of Man is inaccurate.' With this we would agree, except to say that the Book of Daniel speaks of the sufferings of Israel as *the one destined to be* the Son of Man.   [2] See above, p. 97 f.
[3] Mark 14.21 (*bis*), 41.
[4] Mark 8.31; 9.12, 31; 10.33, and 10.45 (partly).
[5] For a refutation of Bultmann's conjecture that this logion was originally a popular proverb transferred to Jesus by the Hellenistic Church see W. Manson, *Mess ah*, p. 60. If it was a proverb, it is just as likely to have been an Aramaic one, applied by Jesus to himself with a deeper meaning—though the person addressed may not have perceived this.

sayings[1] Jesus is urging a would-be follower to count the cost of discipleship. Elsewhere[2] the language used by Jesus is that of bearing the cross. Here he speaks of 'having nowhere to lay his head'. That can hardly have been meant literally, since, at times at least, Jesus was able to stay the night with friends, and no doubt did so whenever possible.[3] To have to spend the night out was doubtless necessary at times when on a journey, but it was not a distinctive part or inseparable condition of his ministry. It is better therefore to take the phrase 'nowhere to lay his head' as a *figurative* expression for rejection. The saying in question therefore comes very close in meaning to the predictions of the Passion, especially to the one at Mark 9.12, which is couched in general terms. To say 'the Son of man hath not where to lay his head' is a figurative and more striking way of saying 'The Son of man must suffer much and be rejected'. Bultmann's second argument against the authenticity of the 'suffering' sayings is that they never speak of the Parousia, while the Parousia sayings never speak of the suffering. This difficulty also is apparent, rather than real, if the Parousia sayings take the suffering for granted, and if the 'suffering' sayings by their very use of the term 'Son of Man' imply the triumph. The Parousia sayings are spoken by Jesus while he was on the way to the cross. This is brought out with particular clarity in the Markan narrative. The Parousia saying in Mark 13.26 occurs in the Little Apocalypse after the Messianic woes which Jesus declares are to be set in motion by his Passion. The Little Apocalypse as it stands is of course composite, but it is certain that Jesus predicted woes first for himself and then his followers. He bids them pray that they may be preserved through temptations.[4] Further, eschatological tribulation, particularly the break up of families, is promised in Matt. 10.34-36, flight from tribulation in Luke 17.31, and martyrdom in Mark 8.34 f, 10.39. All these woes must precede the Parousia, and when Jesus speaks of the coming of the Son of Man he *assumes* that they will precede it. Is it then

[1] Cf. Mark 8.34-37; Matt. 10.38-39 para. [2] See references above, footnote 1.
[3] e.g. Mark 1.29-35 (at Simon's house); 11.11; cf. 12, 19 (Bethany).
[4] πειρασμοί Mark 14.38; cf. Matt. 6.13 para.; for the eschatological significance of this word see Dodd, *Parables*, p. 166, footnote 1.

too much to suppose that he assumes his own suffering in the Parousia sayings? Again, in the suffering Son of Man sayings, even if the mention of the Resurrection has been introduced *post eventum*, the very use of the term Son of Man implies triumph and Parousia.[1] For these reasons therefore, we cannot agree that the notion of a suffering Son of Man is a Markan invention.

What finally of the sayings in group A, which speak of the present activity of Jesus? The difficulty about them is that they all occur in the *public* teaching of Jesus, whereas all the sayings in group B occur in the esoteric teaching given to the disciples. In view of this it is not surprising that many critics tend to regard such sayings as Mark 2.10 and 28 as 'Christian comment'.[2] There is much to be said for this point of view, but it is never advisable to reject sayings in order to make a theory water-tight. If our foregoing argument is correct, there is no need to suppose that the public would have known what Jesus meant by the 'Son of Man'. Jesus had not yet expounded, even to his disciples, the whole Danielic conception of the Son of Man and his relation to that figure. The public would therefore read into it as much as they apprehended of Jesus already, and no more. They would no doubt regard it as a mysterious self-identification used by a prophet precisely as the bearer of the Word of God.[3] In any case, the root of the difficulty lies in the assumption that 'Son of Man' was already current in apocalyptic Judaism as a Messianic title, and would be readily understood as such. And, as we have seen,[4] the only evidence in favour of this assumption is now perceived to be highly questionable. To Jesus, however, it would mean that in declaring the eschatological forgiveness of sin and in dispensing with the Sabbath, he was *proleptically* exercising the functions of the coming Son of Man, just as in his proclamation

[1] See above, p. 102.
[2] Rawlinson, *Mark*, p. 34. Cf. also *ibid.*, p. 24: 'The difficulty lies not in the mere use of the title Son of Man, but in the open and explicit avowal, in the presence of his enemies and in terms which could hardly be misunderstood, of the claim to exercise upon earth a divine privilege'.
[3] Perhaps as in Ezek. 2.1, etc.: this, as we suggested above, p. 99f, may be the element of truth in the 'Ezekiel hypothesis'—it represents not Jesus' intention, but the (inadequate) apprehension of the public.   [4] p. 98.

and healings the powers of the Kingdom were already proleptically at work.

Thus the three apparently divergent uses of the term possess a unity in the mind of our Lord himself. In all of them, Jesus speaks of the Son of Man as an office which he is destined to enter upon as a result of his earthly activity, but an office in which he is proleptically engaged already. The clue to the understanding of the Son of Man lies in our understanding Jesus' conception of the Kingdom of God.

It is often held that Jesus 'conflated' the concepts of the Servant and the Son of Man. This does not, however, exactly express the relationship between the two ideas. It is not that the Servant and the Son of Man are fused into one figure. It is rather that the Servant language, which was rooted in our Lord's conception of divine Sonship as obedience, is used to fill out the Danielic picture of the sufferings of Israel which are the precondition of the triumph of the Son of Man. There are, as it were, two periods in his activity, as Jesus himself saw it. First, there is the period of earthly obedience and suffering, which he conceives in the language of the Servant, and the future period, in which the Kingdom will have come, and which he expresses in terms of the Son of Man. The dividing point between them is the cross, which is as decisive for his person as it is for the Kingdom. We may express Jesus' conception of his person graphically thus:

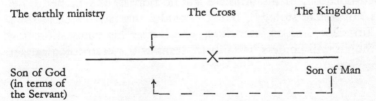

The earthly ministry   The Cross   The Kingdom

Son of God
(in terms of
the Servant)   Son of Man

The cross is the decisive event which sets the eschatological process in motion—the coming of the Reign of God and the triumph of the Son of Man. Yet at the same time, during the earthly ministry, the Kingdom *is dawning*, though it has not yet come. It is active proleptically and in advance. So also Jesus is not yet the Son of Man (which is essentially a triumphant figure). But he acts as the one destined to be the triumphant Son of Man already during his ministry and humiliation. The Kingdom and the Son of Man 'spill over' or 'jut out', as it were, on to this side of the cross, yet the cross itself remains the decisive event which sets both in motion.

Here then we have the lines along which Jesus would appear to have thought about his person. It is not a Christology: it does not involve a 'Messianic consciousness' or a 'Messianic claim'. For neither of the two basic conceptions with which Jesus worked—Son of God and Son of Man—appears to have been commonly accepted as a Messianic title in contemporary Judaism.[1] Both conceptions are, however, images under which the Old Testament expresses the mission and destiny of Israel, the bearer and embodiment of salvation history. Now Jesus of Nazareth knows that he was sent to fulfil the mission and destiny of Israel, to be himself the embodiment and bearer of salvation history at the point of its fulfilment. He does not *claim* himself to be the Son of God; indeed, he studiously avoids the demonstration of such claims as a demonic temptation, but he does know that the Father had declared him to be his Son. Nor does he *claim* to be the Son of Man. He speaks of himself as Son of Man with a certain detachment and reserve, for it speaks to him not of a claim to be asserted, but of a life to be lived, a life of humility and self-oblation even unto death, and, solely on the ground of that humiliation and self-oblation, of his ultimate vindication by the Father. This is not a 'Christology', but it provides the raw materials for a Christology for the later days, when, after his vindication, the Church will confess its faith in Jesus as the eschatological act of God.

4. THE CHRISTOS

With the next two terms, Christos and Kyrios, we pass beyond those interpretations of his person which were constitutive for the mind of Jesus to those which were decisive for the Church's confession of faith after the Resurrection. It is

---

[1] See above, pp. 81 and 98.

noteworthy too, that whereas the former terms which we have been considering (Son of God, Servant and Son of Man) are terms which the Old Testament applies to Israel corporately, the latter are more distinctly individual. And whereas the former ones speak primarily of mission and destiny, the latter speak of authority and fulfilment. Here we have the real difference and tension between the Jesus of History and the *kerygma* of the Church. It is not that the history of Jesus on the one hand is purely prophetic, and the Church's *kerygma* soteriological. It is the difference and tension between present and future, between history in the process of becoming, and history which has been fulfilled. The Christology of the Church is the confession that God *has acted* eschatologically in Jesus. The 'Christology' of Jesus (if we may call it such) is the confession that God is *in the process of accomplishing*, and is about to complete, his eschatological act in him. Clearly then, the Church was not acting arbitrarily in placing this interpretation upon the history of Jesus. There is nothing arbitrary in its ascription to Jesus, after his Resurrection, of the titles Christos and Kyrios, as the description of what he had become through his death. But we may go further than this. Although Jesus does not himself make direct use of these titles for himself, he does as it were set his seal to them and sanction them for later use.

Apart from the use of Christos in the title of Mark's Gospel (where it is a proper name, rather than a title), it occurs first in the Markan narrative at Peter's Confession at Caesarea Philippi[1]:

> And he asked them, But who say ye that I am? Peter answereth and saith unto him, Thou art the Christ. And he charged them that they should tell no man of him. And he began to teach them that the Son of man must suffer.[2] (Mark 8.29-31.)

The reaction of Jesus to Peter's acknowledgement of him is

[1] The addition of $X\rho\iota\sigma\tau\grave{o}\nu$ $\epsilon\tilde{\iota}\nu\alpha\iota$ at Mark 1.34 in B, etc., is probably due to assimilation to the parallel in Luke 4.41.
[2] For a discussion of Bultmann's view that the Petrine confession is a misplaced Resurrection appearance, see above p. 54.

distinctly reserved. He neither accepts it unqualifiedly (as one would expect him to accept it, if the episode were intended to be a post-Resurrection appearance), nor rejects it out of hand. Instead, he charges Peter to tell no man 'of him' (viz., that he is the Christos), and goes on at once to speak of the suffering of the Son of Man. Jesus seems to imply that the title 'Christos' is in some sense predicable of him (it is Peter's word, not his own, but it is correct as far as it goes, and in a certain sense). Everything however turns, not upon the title, but the content. And the title cannot be filled with content until a certain history has been accomplished: 'The Son of man must suffer many things.' After Jesus has suffered those things, and has been exalted as the Son of Man, after he has performed the decisive act which will set the eschatological process in motion, then, and not until then, will it be proper to call Jesus the 'Christos', and to proclaim him before men as the bringer of eschatological salvation.

The next occurrence of Christos in the Markan narrative is at Mark 9.41. The use of Christos here, not as a title, but absolutely as a proper name, is a clear indication that this occurrence is secondary, and moreover, the original form of the saying is almost certainly that given in Matt. 10.42, where in place of 'because ye are Christ's' we have 'in the name of a disciple'.

In the question 'What think ye of Christ?' (Mark 12.35), Jesus is raising what was ostensibly a purely theoretical discussion on Christology, a fact which seems to vouch for the authenticity of this episode. The reply of Jesus indicates that he thought of Christos as a title predicable not of an earthly figure, but of one exalted to the right hand of God. Once again, he does not claim the title for himself in his earthly life. He shelves it for future reference. Time will come, as the next saying will show, when he will be at the right hand of God, and then men will call him the Christos.

Finally there is the answer of Jesus to the High Priest. The historicity of this scene has been widely questioned, especially by the form critics.[1] Yet an acknowledgement

---

[1] e.g. Bultmann, *Tradition*, pp. 290 f.

on the part of Jesus of some sort of Messianic claim is
demanded by the undeniable historical fact that Jesus was
condemned to death as a Messianic pretender (Mark 15.2, 9
and especially 26). To the High Priest's question, Jesus
answers 'I am'. Here he goes beyond the reserve of Caesarea
Philippi, but understandably so, since he is already standing
in the context of his Passion, and there is no longer any chance
of the claim being misunderstood. Moreover, Jesus at once
goes on to qualify his acceptance of the title. The καί with
which he introduces this qualification is, I suggest, the adver-
sative Semitic *wᵉ¹*:'I am, *but* (in the sense that) ye shall see the
Son of Man sitting on the right hand of power, and coming on
the clouds of heaven.' Jesus is the Christos, but only in the
sense that by his humiliation there visible before the eyes of
the High Priest and the Sanhedrin he is destined to be the
triumphant Son of man. Hence the apostolic proclamation is
in perfect harmony with, and has its sanction in, the mind of
the Jesus of History, when it declares that it was at his exaltation that Jesus was '*made* Christos' (Acts 2.36). For it was not
until after the exaltation, not until after the decisive event of
the Passion and death, that Jesus could be said to have entered
on the functions of the Christos. By his history he had filled
the term with a unique, specifically 'Christian' content.

5. THE KYRIOS

It was the belief of the early Church that after his Resurrection Jesus was exalted to the right hand of God as κύριος (Acts
2.36; Phil. 2.9-11). In other words his dignity as Kyrios dates
specifically from his exaltation. Had the use of this title any
sanction in the mind of Jesus himself? Bultmann has revived
Bousset's theory that the use of the term Kyrios as applied to
Jesus was an innovation of the Hellenistic Churches, and
represents an approximation of the Christian theology to
Hellenistic religiosity.[2] The conclusive argument against

---

[1] Matthew evidently took it thus: πλὴν λέγω ὑμῖν (26.64).
[2] *Theology*, p. 51: The arguments of Bousset's *Kyrios Christos* (which has never
been translated into English) are summarized by Rawlinson, *Christ*, pp. 231 ff.

Bousset's theory is the Aramaic liturgical formula *Maranatha*, which Dr. Rawlinson aptly calls the 'Achilles' heel' of Bousset's theory. There is no reason to doubt that this formula arose on Palestinian soil, like all the Aramaic words in the gospels. Secondly, Acts 2.36 occurs in one of the speeches of Acts for which the evidence for an Aramaic source is particularly strong.[1] Thirdly, the expression 'at the right hand of God' has an inalienable place in the primitive preaching (Acts 2.33, 5.31; Rom. 8.34, etc.); it is clearly derived from Ps. 110.1, and the doctrine of the *sessio ad dextram* involves also from that same verse the doctrine of Christ's Lordship. Bultmann admits that *Maranatha* was used as a liturgical formula in the Aramaic-speaking Churches of Palestine, but avers[2] that the term *Maran* could only have been addressed to God, and not to the exalted Jesus. This is a singularly unconvincing attempt to wriggle out of a conclusive argument against his own position. For Bultmann admits himself that the earliest Church expected the coming not simply of God, but precisely of Jesus, whom, after his exaltation, they had come to identify with the Son of Man.[3] Since primitive Christian eschatology invariably spoke elsewhere of a coming of *Jesus* as Christ and Lord rather than of the Father (Acts 3.20; I Thess. 4.16), it is surely unthinkable that *Maran(a)* could have meant any one else but Jesus. Moreover it seems that the Christian use of this word goes back to an honorific title by which Jesus was addressed during his earthly life, and which is reproduced in our gospels by the vocative κύριε.[4] This form of address is attested in Mark only at 7.28, where it is used by the Syro-Phoenician woman, but that it was also used by the disciples of Jesus seems to be well established from the Q logion Matt. 7.21 = Luke 6.46. In later Christian usage the term had of course acquired a new significance: it was no longer a purely honorific designation, but an ascription of Messianic power. How did it undergo this transformation? Partly of course by the impact of events. That

---

[1] Dodd, *Apostolic Preaching*, p. 20. The searching analysis to which Professor H. F. D. Sparks has submitted some of Torrey's alleged Semitisms in Acts 1.1-15.35 in J.T.S. I (new series), Part 1, pp. 16 ff is a warning against undue stress on this argument, but does not seem to affect the kerygmatic speeches in these chapters.
[2] *Theology*, p. 52.　　[3] *Theology*, p. 33, etc.　　[4] Cf. Dalman, *Jesus-Jeshuah*, p. 13.

Jesus, whom the disciples had addressed as *Maran(a)* during his earthly life, the disciples now knew to be exalted at the right hand of God, and therefore the events themselves had filled the address with a deeper meaning. But partly also this enrichment of meaning had, it would appear, the sanction of Jesus himself:

And Jesus answered and said, as he taught in the temple, How say the scribes that the Christ is the son of David? David himself said in the Holy Spirit,
> The Lord said *unto my Lord*,[1]
> Sit thou on my right hand,
> Till I make thine enemies the footstool of thy feet.

David then calleth him Lord; and whence is he his son? (Mark 12.35 ff).

The fact that the primitive Church made such wide use of Ps. 110.1 both in direct quotation as a prophecy fulfilled in Jesus (Acts 2.34) and as the basis of its doctrine of the *sessio ad dextram* makes it easy to suppose that the dialogue of Mark 12.35 ff is a piece of *Gemeindetheologie* put into the mouth of Jesus. On the other hand the situation presupposed by the dialogue and character of its language are wholly compatible with a context in the ministry of Jesus. Jesus is not talking about himself. This is in form an academic discussion about Messianic doctrine, conducted in the approved Rabbinic style. Jesus is speaking of the Messiah as a figure detached from himself, exactly as in those passages in which he speaks in public about the coming Son of Man. Now Jesus also, in his answer to the High Priest at his trial, interpreted Ps. 110.1 as a reference to the Son of Man (Mark 14.62, which combines Dan. 7.13 with Ps. 110.1). Therefore it is clear that Jesus regarded 'Adoni' as an appropriate title, not for himself in his earthly ministry, but for the Son of Man exalted at the right hand of God. Thus Jesus himself sanctions the process by which *Maran(a)* applied to him as a purely honorific title in his earthly life, becomes eventually, through the impact of subsequent events, a title applicable to him as the One exalted

---

[1] Heb. *lǎ'dhoni.*

to the right hand of God.[1] Once more, Jesus is providing the raw materials for the Christological confession of the primitive Church.

6. THE SON OF DAVID

In Rom. 1.3 we are told that the Gospel of God concerned 'his Son, who was born of the seed of David according to the flesh'. This is probably a pre-Pauline kerygmatic formula.[2] The implication of this formula is that the Davidic sonship was a status Jesus possessed during his earthly life, and, as in the infancy narratives, it is linked especially with his Birth. Consequently, the early Church seems to have felt that the title 'Son of David' was applicable not to the exalted Lord, but to the Jesus of History. Had this title, with its restriction to his earthly life, any sanction in the mind and teaching of Jesus himself? It is frequently inferred from the dialogue in Mark 12.35-37 that Jesus discountenanced the use of Son of David altogether on the ground of its political implications. The legitimacy of this inference is however open to question. For, as we have seen,[3] the dialogue is an academic discussion on Messianic doctrine. In it Jesus asserts that the Messiah is no merely earthly figure of history, but the Lord exalted to the right hand of God. The implication is that 'Son of David' is a wholly inadequate title for the exalted Lord. Thus Jesus explicitly discourages the application of the title Son of David to himself after his exaltation. But it does not mean that he rejected the use of it to describe certain aspects of his mission on earth. True, he never openly claimed to be the Son of David, but this is on all fours with his attitude to the other titles. He never directly claimed to be the Son of God or the Servant of the Lord or the Christ, and he used the title Son of Man with a distinct reserve and detachment. Yet when blind

---

[1] Those parables which speak of a κύριος and his δοῦλοι (e.g. Mark 13.34; Luke 12.35-40, 42-48 para.) probably contain a similar sanction. Bultmann considers that these parables are products of the Church (*Tradition*, p. 125), produced when it was wrestling with the problems of a delayed Parousia. But see Kümmel, *Verheissung*, p. 48, footnote 114.
[2] Cf. Dodd, *Apostolic Preaching*, p. 14.   [3] Above, p. 113.

Bartimaeus greeted him as the Son of David he was not re-buffed (Mark 10.47-48), nor was the multitude which hailed him as the harbinger of 'the kingdom of our father David' (Mark 11.10; Matthew has altered the greeting to: 'Hosanna to the Son of David' (21.9) thus bringing out the implication of the Markan version). Jesus does not therefore appear to have rejected the title. Is it possible that he believed himself to be of Davidic descent, and saw in that fact something of importance for the understanding of his mission? Now the very presence of the term 'Son of David' in the *kerygma* suggests that its application to Jesus was not an invention of the early Church. For unlike the titles which refer to the exalted Jesus, it is not a confession of faith, but rather the necessary precondition of a confession of faith. For unless Jesus was of Davidic descent, no Jew could have accepted him as the Messiah. Hence its place in the *kerygma*. But if it was to secure conviction, there must have been plausible grounds for its assertion. In other words, it must have been a known fact that Jesus was of Davidic descent, or at least came of a family which preserved a tradition of such descent. That such a tradition existed is by no means improbable, since the ancient Jews kept family trees with the same assiduity as the modern Welsh. Many a modern Welsh family claims descent from Hywel Dda or some other ancient Prince, and many an ancient Jewish family must have cherished similar claims. Moreover, Eusebius[1] informs us that other members of Jesus' family claimed descent from the royal line. It may well be therefore that Jesus grew up in a family where the tradition of Davidic descent was a source of understandable pride. Perhaps it was just this which, humanly speaking, led Jesus to reflect on his life's mission. A study of the prophecies of the scion of the royal line in Isa. 9 and 11 would have led him on to the Servant of the later chapters of Isaiah, linked as it is to the earlier figure by the endowment with the Spirit.[2] Once this conflation of the two figures was established, the way was open for a reading

---

[1] Eccles. *History*, III, p. 20.
[2] Cf. Isa. 42.1, 61.1 with Isa. 11.1: Jesus of course knew nothing of Deutero- and Trito-Isaiah!

of the Psalms (whose Davidic authorship was unquestioned, Mark 12.36) as a further pattern for his mission and destiny. The cry from the cross (Mark 15.34 = Ps. 22.1, hardly an invention of the Church) suggests that his mind had worked along these lines. We conclude therefore that while the title Son of David was not a dominant conception for Jesus, it nevertheless played a significant part in the interpretation of his historical mission and destiny, and as such came to have a legitimate place in that part of the *kerygma* which dealt with his earthly life.

7. SUMMARY

'The life of Jesus was un-Messianic'—such was Bultmann's conclusion about the Jesus of History. At best this statement conserves an important half-truth. The life of Jesus was un-Messianic in any sense of that term previously recognized in Jewish eschatological hope. The life of Jesus was un-Messianic in the sense that Jesus never proclaimed himself to be Messiah. The life of Jesus was un-Messianic in the sense that Jesus did not possess what modern critics have called a 'Messianic consciousness' or make a 'Messianic claim' (except perhaps right at the end, at the supreme, paradoxical moment of his humiliation). The life of Jesus was un-Messianic in the sense that he did not impose a Christology upon his disciples. But what was the life of Jesus? It was a life wrought out in conscious obedience to the eschatological will of God, a life in which proclamation of the impending advent of the Reign of God and the performance of the signs which heralded its approach culminated in the suffering of the cross as the decisive event by which the eschatological process should be inaugurated. Was that life un-Messianic? It would be truer to say that it was 'pre-Messianic', for it was the outcome of the lowly history of Jesus that he was, in the belief of the Church, exalted to be the Messiah.

Jesus was concerned, as we have said, not so much to impose a Christology upon his disciples, as to evoke from them the response of faith in God's eschatological action in him. Jesus did not himself formulate that response for his disciples, but he did provide them with the raw materials out of which they would later formulate their response. The proclamation of Jesus and the *kerygma* of the Church are by no means identical, but neither are they incompatible. The proclamation of Jesus proclaims that God *is about to act* decisively and eschatologically in him, the Church's *kerygma* proclaims that *he has so acted*.

We have not demonstrated the ultimate truth of the *kerygma*. That, as we saw at the outset, is not the task of the historian. But we have, we may hope, performed the humble, preliminary task of showing that the Church's *kerygma* is not an arbitrary interpretation imposed upon an arbitrarily selected stretch of history, but that it has an intelligible basis in that history, and in the mind of the chief participator in it. Whether the Church's *kerygma* is ultimately true, however, is still a matter for the hearer of that *kerygma* to decide.

V

EPILOGUE: THE EMERGENCE
OF THE ECCLESIA

Parturient montes, nascetur ridiculus mus—such is the verdict which not only the cynic and the unbeliever, but even the candid historian might be tempted to pass on the history of Jesus of Nazareth. He had proclaimed the imminence of the cosmic End, and had claimed himself to perform the decisive event which would bring it about. But the outcome, so far as the historian can see, is the emergence of the *ecclesia* and its *kerygma*. Are we then still left with a fundamental difference between the intention of Jesus and the interpretation of his history in the Church's proclamation? Was the Church compelled, in the light of subsequent facts, to revise and adjust its estimate of Jesus and his achievement, so that in place of the cosmic End the Church itself became the intention and outcome of the history of Jesus? The difficulty is eased considerably as soon as it is observed that Jesus explicitly allowed for an interval between the performance of the decisive event and the consummation of the End. The death of Jesus would inaugurate for his disciples a period characterized by witness to him (Matt. 10.32 para.; Mark 13.10, 14.9), by trials before secular authorities (Mark 13.9), by persecution and even martyrdom (Mark 10.38). Some of the disciples, however, would survive this period and be still alive when the Kingdom of God came with power (Mark 9.1). During this period also the disciples would assemble for the celebration of the *anamnesis* of the Christian Exodus, which for them would replace the *anamnesis* of the Mosaic Exodus in the Jewish passover. There is thus abundant testimony of very different kinds in the various strata of the gospel tradition that Jesus allowed for an interval between his death and the coming of the End. Given this interval, we have the recognition by Jesus of the emergence of the *ecclesia* (in fact if not in name), as an essential

118

part of the outcome of his work. The *ecclesia* belongs to the interim between the cross and the End.

But the interim period is qualitatively different from the time which preceded it, including the time of Jesus' ministry. For during the ministry the decisive event of the cross still lay in the future. True, the powers of the coming Kingdom could already make themselves felt in advance in the healings and exorcisms of Jesus. But after the cross, the powers of the Kingdom are operative in a wholly different way. Before, they were active in producing signs of the future event, now they are active in *mediating* the power released by that event. This power is mediated by the *kerygma* and the sacraments, which are essentially different from the healings and exorcisms of Jesus. The miracles of Jesus had a *future* orientation, pointing forward to the decisive event of the cross. The *kerygma* and the sacraments are orientated primarily towards the *past*. The burden of the *kerygma* is in the main what God *has done* in Jesus. Baptism is performed in the name of *Jesus*, that is to say, it brings a man into intimate relationship with the past event of the death and Resurrection of Jesus. The Eucharist is the showing forth of the past event of the Lord's death. The Spirit is the Spirit of Jesus, of him who raised up Jesus. All the phenomena of the Church's life are thus related primarily to the past, and reproduce the power of the decisive event of the past in the present. To this extent, therefore, it is legitimate to speak of 'realized eschatology' after the cross and Resurrection as it was not before. But at this point we must be cautious. There is still a future, which, though not a decisive future, is still necessary. For the realization of eschatology is partial and hidden even after Easter and Pentecost. The life of the *ecclesia* is hid with Christ in God, and it does not yet appear what it will be. The *kerygma* speaks also of the return of Christ. Baptism seals a man unto the day of redemption. The Eucharist shows forth the death of Christ *till he come*. The Spirit is also the ἀπαρχή and the ἀρραβών of the final glory. Yet, as Professor Cullmann has insisted,[1] this does not mean that the decisive event still lies in the future. For the Church places the de-

[1] *Christ and Time*, 1951, esp. pp. 81-93.

119

cisive event exactly where Jesus himself had placed it, namely at his death and exaltation. For the *kerygma*, as for Jesus himself, *that* is the decisive event which sets the eschatological process in motion, and of which the Church and all its activity are a part.

It is not therefore possible to drive a wedge between the proclamation of Jesus and the proclamation of the Church here. The sole difference between them is that whereas for Jesus the decisive event is still in the near future, for the Church the decisive event now lies in the past.

But there is one last difficulty which must be faced. Both Jesus, apparently,[1] and the early Church certainly, were mistaken in supposing that the interval between the decisive event of the cross and its final consummation would be a brief one, at the most a matter of decades. This error, however, as Professor Cullmann points out,[2] 'is explained on a psychological basis in the same way that we explain the hasty determinations of the date of the end of the war when once the conviction is present that the decisive battle has already taken place.' *Qualitatively*, both Jesus and the early Church were, in the perspective of Christian faith, correct in their division of time. The decisive event of the cross inaugurates the interim period of church history, followed by the final consummation. The rightness or wrongness of the perspective of Christian faith is, however, not a matter for the historian to decide. His sole concern is to establish the substantial identity between the *kerygma* of Jesus and the *kerygma* of the earliest Church. The only difference between them is that whereas for Jesus the decisive event lies in the immediate future, for the Church that event lies in the past.

[1] It is possible of course that Jesus was accommodating himself to the only (mythological) imagery which was available to him in order to explain the decisive character of his achievement, but this question is raised by *a priori* considerations which are beyond the province of the historian.
[2] *Christ and Time*, pp. 87 f.

INDEX OF NAMES

Index of Names

Rengstorf, K. H., 86n
Richardson, A., 20n, 35n(2), 37n

Schlatter, A., 90n, 93n
Schniewind, J., 61n, 70n, 71n, 90n
Schrenk, G., 31n, 87n
Schweitzer, A., 74
Smith, B. T. D., 45n
Sparks, H. F. D., 69n, 112n
Strack, H. L., *see* Billerbeck
Streeter, B. H., 86n, 97n

Taylor, V., 16n, 20n, 27n, 38n, 41n,
  44n, 45n, 57n, 59n, 61f, 62n, 70,
  75f, 86n, 87n, 95n
Torrey, C. C., 112
Turner, C. H., 87n

Weiss, J., 59
Wellhausen, J., 62
Wrede, W., 19

INDEX OF BIBLICAL REFERENCES

Index of Biblical References

Index of Biblical References

Index of Biblical References

Bible Ref.	Page	Bible Ref.	Page
Romans		**Colossians**	
8.34	112	2.12	60
9.31	26		
13.12	23	**I Thessalonians**	
		1.10	26
I Corinthians		2.16	26 (2)
ch. 11	67, 68	4.15	26
11.23-25	65 f, 72 n	4.15-17	28
11.23	65 and n	4.16	112
11.24b	72 n		
15.3	65 n	**I Timothy**	
15.8	88	5.1,2,11,14	57 n
15.11	60		
15.43	27	**Hebrews**	
15.51	28	1.5	87
		4.10	101
II Corinthians		5.5	87
3.6	76 n	10.25	23
3.6 ff	65 n	13.7	57 n
5.17	76 n	13.17	57 n
10.14	26	13.24	57 n
11.32 f	66		
		James	
Galatians		5.8	23
1.1	66		
1.15	88	**I Peter**	
1.15-17	66 (2)	4.7	23
1.16	66	5.5	57 n
1.17	66		
4.24 ff	65 n	**II Peter**	
6.15	76 n	1.17	53
Ephesians		**I John**	
2.15	76	1.7	43
4.24	76		
		Revelation	
Philippians		2.27	87
2.6	39	12.5	87
2.7-8	17	12.9	27
2.9	17	19.15	87
2.9-11	111		
2.11	17		
3.16	26		